MAKING SHAKER
WOODENWARE

KERRY PIERCE

Sterling Publishing Co., Inc.
New York, NY

Acknowledgments

Variations of the chapters "Shaker Production Run," on introducing variety, and "In the Shaker Manner," about the work of Charles Harvey, appeared in *Woodwork* magazine.
The measured drawings of Shaker woodenware are the work of Kevin Pierce.
The drawings of hands at work are the work of the author.

Library of Congress Cataloging-in-Publication Data
Pierce, Kerry.
Making Shaker woodenware / Kerry Pierce.
ISBN 0-8069-3178-7
Data on File

Book Design by Judy Morgan
Edited by R. Neumann

1 3 5 7 9 10 8 6 4 2
Published by Sterling Publishing Company, Inc.
387 Park Avenue South, New York, N.Y. 10016
© 1998 by Kerry Pierce
Distributed in Canada by Sterling Publishing
℅ Canadian Manda Group, One Atlantic Avenue, Suite 105
Toronto, Ontario, Canada M6K 3E7
Distributed in Great Britain and Europe by Cassell PLC
Wellington House, 125 Strand, London WC2R 0BB, England
Distributed in Australia by Capricorn Link (Australia) Pty Ltd.
P.O. Box 6651, Baulkham Hills, Business Centre, NSW 2153, Australia
Printed in Hong Kong

I would like to express my appreciation to
the following individuals:

Will, Robin, Bert, Ian, Weeds, B.J., Dave, and Joe
Rob, Jessica, Sarah, Kyla, and Courtney
Emily
Andy
Elaine, first and foremost.

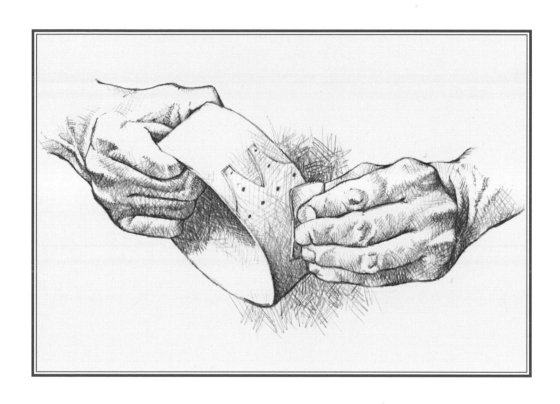

CONTENTS

PREFACE

In planning this book, I tried to focus on some of the simpler Shaker forms, pieces requiring only a few board feet of lumber and a relatively modest amount of shop time.

This scale permits the woodworker—even the individual on a budget—to make extensive use of figured wood, something the Shakers, too, often did with great success, marrying simple forms to lushly figured material. Also, the book presents pieces that can be made in a weekend or two, so that the moment of inspiration is not separated from the contemplation of the completed work by many months.

Each of the projects is represented by a color photo of the finished piece (my reproduction, not the original), and by a measured drawing, a materials list, and a brief discussion of the construction process. Where necessary, I've included photo sequences detailing tricky procedures.

While the book doesn't offer a discussion of every step in the execution of every project—some experience is assumed—it should provide a useful guide to the construction of the twenty forms presented here.

In addition, I've included information about the Shakers and their approach to woodworking. This is for the purpose of providing a historical context for the modern woodworker who chooses to reproduce Shaker forms, a reminder that none of us works in isolation, that we are all a part of a woodworking continuum that extends back for hundreds of years.

Kerry Pierce

INTRODUCTION

I started work on Making Shaker Woodenware by going through some of my favorite books—John Kassay's The Book of Shaker Furniture, the four Ejner Handberg collections of measured drawings, and other books—marking what I saw as exemplary pieces.

Next, I went to the library and procured, through interlibrary loan, a pair of books by June Sprigg and Jim Johnson devoted specifically to Shaker woodenware. Although intended for collectors rather than builders, these two books—Shaker Woodenware: A Field Guide, *Volumes 1 and 2*—were valuable sources of forms, some of which I had never before seen. Once again, I marked exemplary pieces.

At this point, I began to impose some kind of organization onto the pieces I had selected. Early on, I eliminated any coopered work—buckets, pails, etc.—because of the specialized tools and skills coopering requires.

I almost eliminated the oval boxes for the same reason, but after considering the matter for several weeks, I decided that no book on this subject would be complete without oval boxes, since they are the quintessential examples of Shaker woodenware.

Fortunately, the field of Shaker woodenware is deep and rich, offering a wide variety of attractive forms, even when coopered pieces are removed

from consideration. Pared down and organized into four categories—the kitchen, the sewing room, the work room, and the storage room—these were what I felt was a very strong collection of objects with which to work.

After assembling the tiny step-stool (see page 78) and applying the first coat of finish, I placed it on a sheet of plywood laid across a pair of sawhorses that I'd set up to provide a stage on which recently finished pieces could dry. Later, while ripping boards to width for another piece, I bumped the plywood, which jostled the step-stool, knocking it to the floor. When I retrieved the stool, I found not only the expected dings—which could be steamed out and sanded smooth—I also found that the top step had partially separated from the legs.

This would never have happened if the legs had been joined to the top with, for example, wedged-through tenons, a style of joinery common to many similar Shaker pieces.

I therefore resolved that—even though it was my original intention to reproduce every aspect of the Shaker originals (with the already noted exception of material)—I would no longer use nailed butt joints in a key structural element.

Yes, I would continue to use nails in applications where such fasteners are appropriate, as is the case with the bottoms of the tiny dovetailed carriers (these carriers are too small to carry a heavy load). But if a piece would be stronger and more useful with a set of dovetails or mortise-and-tenon joinery, I would include those changes, even if the changes were unfaithful to the Shaker original.

By this decision, no disrespect is intended to the Shaker craftsmen who made the original pieces. These craftsmen were extremely capable, but they built to serve a different set of needs than those I address in my shop. Where I was looking to build pieces intended to last in my twentieth-century American home (complete with children), the Shaker craftsmen built pieces meant to last in the disciplined environment of an insular communal society, a society largely without children.

Ultimately, I also found myself making other changes from the originals for purely aesthetic reasons. For example, in building the two-compartment dining tray, I first decided—for structural reasons—to substitute dovetail and dado joinery for the simple nailed butt joints used on the original. Then, however, as I thought about the tray's bottom, other considerations arose. True, nailing it to a frame strengthened by classical joinery would provide the bottom with sufficient strength to carry any load that might be placed within the tray's two compartments, but how would that bottom board look? On the original, it was nailed to the sides and ends, then simply planed flush all around. On a piece having a frame assembled with nailed butt joints, that would have been appropriate. But on a piece having a frame assembled with dovetails, would such a crude bottom really look right?

I decided it would not. I decided then to make the bottom ⅛ inch larger all around and then, with a plane, to round over that extra ⅛ inch. This molded effect would, I felt, dress up the piece, giving the bottom a look more consistent with the joinery of the frame.

Similarly, as I worked my way through other projects, I made other small changes from the originals to suit my own personal tastes.

I apologize in advance to those purists who believe-perhaps quite rightly—that reproductions of furniture and woodenware should mimic every aspect of the original—right down to the species of wood, the type of finish, and the presence of tool marks. This book is not intended for those purists. It is, instead, intended for those woodworkers who, like myself, are drawn to the clean lines and imaginative design of Shaker woodenware but who wish to reproduce it in ways suitable to their own tastes.

· THE SHAKERS ·

SIMPLICITY. HARMONY. BEAUTY.

From our current perspective, in the last days of the twentieth century, simplicity, harmony, and beauty are the qualities we see when looking back at the nineteenth-century Shakers. The visual imagery that has shaped our perspective is powerfully evocative. For example, the photos illustrating June Sprigg and David Larkin's book, Shaker Life, Work, and Art, *portray calm, carefully arranged, and well-lit Shaker interiors, in which the material accoutrements of Shaker life—dishes, tools, baskets, boxes—are laid out with the kind of effortless precision to which we all aspire in our own lives.*

Charles Harvey

However, that view of the Shakers—although truthful—is not the only truthful view of this nineteenth-century American phenomenon, for their history was, in its early years, also marked by persecution, by violence, and by material impoverishment.

ENGLAND

In 1758, the founder of the Shakers, Mother Ann Lee—an uneducated laborer from Manchester, England—joined a group of dissident Quakers led by James and Jane Wardley. Perhaps because her personal life was so unhappy—all four of her children died at very young ages—Ann Lee threw herself into her religion, soon becoming one of the leading figures in the Wardley group, a group known as the Shaking Quakers because of their tendency to shake when imbued with the Holy Spirit.

In 1770, while in an English jail for disrupting the Sabbath, Ann Lee had a vision in which the fundamental principles that would ultimately guide the American Shaker movement became clear to her.

Celibacy was the first and most important of these principles. In her view, much of the suffering that humans endured could be attributed to the exercise of sexuality. She decided then to advocate a new approach to life, one in which men and women related to one another with the innocence of children, undisturbed by the power of lust. The sexually segregated living arrangement characteristic of American Shaker communities is one result of this belief.

Equality was another of the Shaker themes to evolve during this period. Ann Lee took the then radical view that everyone—regardless of sex, race, and age—was equal in the eyes of the Lord. And this was a concept that she and her followers actually put into practice here on earth. In fact, in the many Shaker communities that later took root on American soil, women ranked as high or, in some cases, higher than did the men.

Simplicity in all things—most particularly in all material things—was another of the Shaker themes to become clarified during this period, and it is this concept that later gave the products of Shaker industry their defining quality. Meeting houses, machines, woodwork—all were designed with an elegant simplicity, one in which form closely followed function, and one in which the human desire to apply ornament was kept under a tight rein.

Later, during another English imprisonment, Mother Ann had a vision in which she saw her ideals flourishing on the American continent, and the next spring, on May 19, 1774, she and a group of loyal followers—including her husband, Abraham Stanley, and her brother, William Lee—set sail from Liverpool, England, for New York.

Opposite: (1930) Sister Sarah Collins weaves a chair seat in her workroom. Notice the clamp in which the chair is held, presenting the seat at a convenient working height. It is equipped with a swivel which permits the chair to be turned upside down in order to weave the bottom of the seat.

During the last decades of the nineteenth century and the first decades of the twentieth, the Shaker chairmaking operation at New Lebanon, New York, slowly collapsed, as the men and women who had worked in this field grew old and died. In its final years, the Mt. Lebanon facility was operated by two women: Sister Lillian Barlow and Sister Sarah Collins. Sister Lillian died in 1942, Sister Sarah five years later, bringing this once thriving business to an end.
(Courtesy of the New York State Museum, Albany, New York)

NEW YORK

Failure and disappointment marked Ann's first years in America. Without the money needed to start the kind of community she had envisioned, the members of her group had to separate and find jobs. Ann took work as a washerwoman, but she earned barely enough to pay for food. Then, shortly after their arrival in New York-because of Ann's commitment to celibacy—her husband left her.

When it seemed that the situation could get no worse for Ann and her followers, they heard of a tract of land for sale near Albany, New York. Three members of the group then traveled to this land and, after inspecting it, bought 200 acres.

This was Watervliet, which would become the site of the first Shaker community.

However, although they finally had a place in which to pursue Ann's vision, their struggles were not yet over. Three years after

buying the land, they erected their first communal home—only to watch that home burn to the ground, leaving the group with the dispiriting task of starting all over again. Adding to their misery was the fact that, after five hard years in America, they hadn't attracted a single convert.

But finally, in 1780, their patience and persistence began to pay off. Joseph Meacham, a Baptist minister, took an interest in Ann Lee and her vision. He accepted Ann's statement that she and Christ were the spiritual parents of mankind. He then converted, bringing with him most of his Baptist congregation. Others soon followed.

But this success did not come without a price, for the authorities, their attention drawn by the success of Ann's proselytizing, began to take an interest. And once again Ann Lee found herself in jail, this time in her adopted land of America.

Released in December of 1780, Ann went right back to work. To quicken the pace of conversion, she and her brother William undertook a missionary expedition through New York and several neighboring states, which lasted more than two years. In some locations, Ann was received as a spiritual leader and treated

Dipper. Circa 1830–1845.
Attributed to Giles Bushnell Avery (1815–1890)
New Lebanon, New York. Birch, white pine, maple,
iron, copper. 6½ x 10½ x 4⅝ inches.

(From the collection of Hancock Shaker Village,
Pittsfield, Massachusetts.
Photo: Paul Rocheleau)

with respect. In others, she was victimized and assaulted by angry mobs. Finally, worn down by the strain of travel and missionary work, she returned to the home of Joseph Meacham, and a year later, at the age of forty-eight, saddened by the death of her brother a month earlier, Ann Lee died, well before the society she had founded reached its zenith.

idea of the communal settlement. Up until this time, converts had continued to live in their own homes. But Father Joseph and Mother Lucy decided that another level of separation was required, to protect adherents from the temptations of the outside world. Therefore, at New Lebanon, New York, east of Albany, they began to organize a communal society.

JOSEPH AND LUCY

Before her death, Ann Lee had identified two individuals who had, in her view, special talents. One was Joseph Meacham, the former Baptist minister. The other was Lucy Wright. Within three years of Ann Lee's death, these two individuals had taken control of the Shaker movement and they had begun to put in place structures that would shape the future for the thousands who would ultimately be converted.

The first and most radical of these structures was the

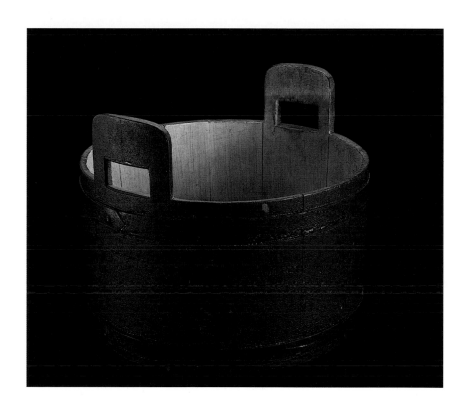

Tub. Circa 1850.
Probably Harvard or Shirley, Massachusetts.
White pine, paint, iron.
9½ x 12⅜ x 11⅞ inches.

(From the collection of Hancock Shaker Village,
Pittsfield, Massachusetts.
Photo: Paul Rocheleau)

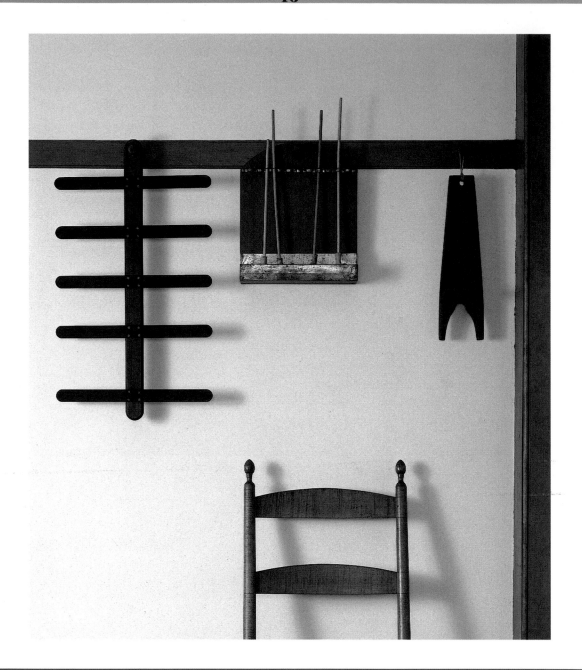

Peg Rail and Accessories.

Five-armed Clothes Hanger. Circa 1860–1880.
Probably Hancock, Massachusetts.
White pine, copper. 27¾ x 15¾ x ½ inches.

Pipe Rack and Pipes. Circa 1840–1860.
Probably Watervliet, New York.White pine, tin-plat-
ed iron, birch, brass, clay. 14 x 11⅜ x 3 inches.

Boot Jack. Circa 1800–1850.
New Lebanon, New York.
Birch, iron. 16⅛ x 4¼ x 1⅞ inches.

(From the collection of Hancock Shaker Village,
Pittsfield, Massachusetts.
Photo: Paul Rocheleau)

The first step in this process was the relocation of about 100 Believers to the adjoining farms of other Believers. At these communal locations, material possessions were shared. Then, finally, a communal dwelling was built, thus beginning the most important of the Shaker communities.

Over the next decade, Father Joseph and Mother Lucy developed a number of additional structures for the expression of Shaker life. One was a system of orders, identifying various levels of commitment to the Shaker faith. Others included the covenant, a document expressing commitment to the Shaker movement that all converts would be asked to sign. Father Joseph and Mother Lucy also helped codify laws concerning Shaker business and government. Additionally, Father Joseph made changes in the ways that Shakers expressed themselves during worship, eliminating the wild shaking and leaping that had originally given the movement its name. He substituted, instead, a much more restrained and formal dance that could be practiced by anyone, at any age, regardless of their physical condition.

In 1796, Father Joseph died. For the next quarter century—the period of the greatest expansion of the movement—Mother Lucy led the Shakers.

On New Year's Day of 1805, she directed three brethren to begin a missionary journey through Ohio and Kentucky and Indiana. This was in response to a prophesy made by Mother Ann Lee that another revival would take place in the West. The trip was enormously successful, resulting in the establishment of nine new Shaker communities— in Ohio, Kentucky, Indiana, and western New York. By the time she died in 1821, Mother Lucy was the head of a society that had sixteen different communities, spread out over eight states, with over 2000 adherents.

Then, during the next two decades three additional communities were founded, and the total number of Shakers rose to over 6000.

It was during this period that the prodigious output of the Shaker industry—particularly its woodworking—began to make its appearance on the American scene. Although there are some documentary references to chair sales during the last decade of the eighteenth century, it was not until the early years of the nineteenth century that the selling of chairs, oval boxes, brooms, sieves, and spinning wheels became widespread.

Initially, the wooden items produced in Shaker communities were intended for the exclusive use of the Shakers themselves. But later, to generate income, surplus goods were allowed to be sold to the outside world. Perhaps the two most important items sold to outsiders were the chairs and the oval boxes. The chairs were manufactured by the thousands at the New Lebanon facility, and oval boxes were also made by the thousands at a number of Shaker communities.

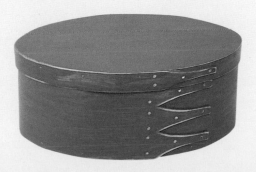

THE DECLINE

In time, the Shaker movement began to falter. The commitment to celibacy was certainly one element in this decline.

Unlike the practitioners of other, more mainstream faiths, the Shakers didn't generate children, who could be trained in their ideology. Too, celibacy required an act of sublimation, which many—who might otherwise have found the faith attractive—just could not or would not manage. Also, the American nation's social policies toward orphans changed in the closing decades of the nineteenth century. States began to write laws governing the adoption process, and other churches, as well as secular organizations, took a more active role in caring for society's orphans. These changes robbed the Shakers of one of their most important sources of new converts.

During the second half of the nineteenth century, the material poverty that had once made Shaker life so appealing to so many became less widespread. The poor and the dispossessed no longer came to Shaker communities willing to trade the religions in which they'd been raised for food, shelter, and security, and, in addition, many committed Shakers found their faith tested by the temptations of the emerging American cities.

By 1960, seventeen communities had closed their doors, and only a handful of Shakers remained in the last two Shaker communities, Canterbury Shaker Village in New Hampshire, which closed its doors to converts in 1965, and the community at Sabbathday Lake in Maine.

CHAPTER TWO

SHAKER
■ WOODWORK ■

In the early years of the American Shaker movement, the woodwork done in the Shaker communities was indistinguishable from the woodwork done outside those communities by non-Shaker crafts-men. After all, those early Shaker woodworkers were simply converts who brought with them the tools and techniques for the construction of furniture and woodenware that they had learned in the outside world.

However, in those first decades of the nineteenth century, the work of Shaker craftsmen began to express, in a very conscious way, the tenets of the Shaker faith. Historical records make it clear that this expression was mandated by the religious leaders during those early years. One—Joseph Meacham, Mother Ann's successor—left writings which explicitly stated the importance of plainness and simplicity in all Shaker goods.

As a result, at the same time that woodworkers in the outside world were laboring to produce the florid forms of American Empire furniture, the Shakers were, in the construction of their furniture, stripping away ornament, striving for ever greater levels of simplicity. In the wrong hands, this removal of ornament would have resulted in crudity, but the Shakers were blessed with many gifted craftsmen who managed to turn the process of simplification into refinement rather than mere elimination.

Few pieces of identifiably Shaker furniture and woodenware exist from the first decades of the nineteenth century. But even in the case of the oldest of those survivors—a chest of drawers presumably made at New Lebanon in 1809—the simple geometry that characterizes much later work is present. Six small half-width drawers, arranged in two columns, stand above six large full-width drawers, which, in turn, stand on a simple plinth with four bracket feet. A molded edge marks the transition from plinth to chest, but otherwise the piece exhibits the severe geometry of a Piet Mondrian painting.

This severity continues unabated throughout the first half of the nineteenth century. There are, for example, many nineteenth century Shaker chests built with similar drawer arrangements and with similar proportions. Some were built-in, a commonly employed tactic; others, like the New Lebanon piece, were freestanding.

Although forms—the tripod table with curved legs, for example—were borrowed from the outside world, those forms were reinterpreted in light of the Shaker aesthetic. While the tripod tables built in the outside world likely featured an elaborately turned (and perhaps carved) pedestal, as well as carved feet, the Shaker pedestal table often featured plainly turned pedestals tapering from bottom to top in a single undisturbed line. However, just as the fancier tables built in the outside world might have incorporated the technically demanding sliding dovetail joint as a way of fastening the legs to the pedestal, so too did the visually simpler Shaker examples. To the Shakers, quality of construction was essential, although ornament was not.

In the closing decades of the nineteenth century, as membership in the various communities began to decline, so too did the aesthetic singularity of much Shaker woodwork, as it began to take on the

Opposite: Delmer Wilson is pictured here, in his shop, in front of the 1083 carriers he made during the winter of 1922–23.

Wilson, who grew up in the Sabbathday Lake Community of Shakers after having been placed there by his mother at age eight, became an accomplished practitioner of many arts and crafts. This diversity wasn't uncommon among Shaker craftsmen. Many highly skilled cabinetmakers were also beekeepers, masons, carpenters, and so on. (Collection of The United Society of Shakers, Sabbathday Lake, Maine)

characteristics of work done in the outside world. Thomas Fisher (1823–1902), working at the Enfield, Connecticut, community of Shakers, produced a large quantity of furniture bearing the unmistakable stamp of the Victorian style, much of it executed in oak, a wood that saw little use in the construction of classic Shaker furniture and woodenware, although it was the preferred material for much of the Victorian furniture then being manufactured in the outside world. Brother Thomas' work features large and ornate cast pulls, molded edges on tabletops and drawer lips, and liberal use of applied moldings. Henry Green (1844–1931), working in the Alfred, Maine, Shaker community at about the same time, also produced work in which the influence of the outside world is clear-

Oval Carriers.
(Top) Circa 1860–1880.
 Probably Canterbury, New Hampshire.
 Birch, white pine, hickory, stain, copper.
7½ x 11⅛ x 8 inches.

(Bottom) Circa 1850–1870.
New Lebanon, New York.
 Birch, white pine, ash, copper.
7 x 15 x 12¼ inches.

(From the collection of Hancock Shaker Village, Pittsfield, Massachusetts.
Photo: Paul Rocheleau)

ly visible. Several writing desks attributed to Brother Henry exhibit elaborately turned spindles and fancy fretwork.

Although still executed with the skill typical of classical Shaker furniture, this hybrid work is less satisfying to contemplate than the Shaker work done in the first half of the nineteenth century by earlier craftsmen; it speaks less directly of the order and restraint that informed earlier Shaker woodwork.

But not all Shaker forms produced in the latter decades of the Society's prominence were tainted by the aesthetics of the outside world. Some forms retained their simplicity and directness well into the twentieth century. One example of this can be found in the oval boxes and carriers made by Delmer Wilson (1873–1961).

The black-and-white photo on page 20, taken in 1923, shows Brother Delmer standing in front of 1083 bentwood carriers made by him during the previous winter. Like their predecessors, these carriers feature a simple oval shape created by bending a softened length of thin wood around a form, which holds it in place through the use of copper tacks that are dri-

ven through fingers cut on one end of the length of wood. The carriers are then completed with a bottom tacked inside the oval, and the addition of a hoop handle, the ends of which are riveted into the carriers' sidewalls.

Spit Box (front). Circa 1840–1860.
New Lebanon, New York.
Sugar maple, white pine, stain, copper.
3¼ x ⅞ inches.

(From the collection of Hancock Shaker Village, Pittsfield, Massachusetts.
Photo: Paul Rocheleau)

Although made in 1923, these carriers would have fit comfortably into a collection of bentwood carriers made seventy-five years earlier.

At its best, Shaker furniture and woodenware offers a concrete expression of the simplicity Mother Ann Lee identified as an essential characteristic of the movement she founded. A chest of drawers was intended to provide brothers or sisters with a place to store clothing. A dipper was intended to bring water from a bucket to the lips. A scoop was intended to bring flour from a bin to a mixing bowl. Any design that failed to recognize the primacy of these functions was deemed inappropriate, and it is this powerful integration of form and function that, even today, even for those of us who are firmly entrenched in the outside world, has given Shaker furniture and woodenware its elegant dignity.

Dipper. Circa 1800–1850.
Unidentified community.
Unidentified wood, possibly
butternut or elm, paint.
3 x 7¼ x 5⅛ inches.
(From the collection of
Hancock Shaker Village,
Pittsfield, Massachusetts.
Photo: Paul Rocheleau)

CHAPTER THREE

▪ TOOLS ▪

Twenty-five years ago, when I first decided to try my hand at wood-working, my wife and I were living in a 26fi-foot-long travel trailer. Although it would have been spacious for a family of Lilliputians, for two average-sized contemporary Americans it was cramped. Yes, two friends could drop in after supper, but unless we wanted to press in beside them at the tiny dinette, my wife and I had to sit on the floor.

There simply wasn't room for a woodworking shop. Even if I had gutted the trailer and my wife and I had slept in the yard, there wouldn't have been enough space, at least for the minimum shop space requirements described in the woodworking press.

And in my efforts to become a woodworker, I faced one other obstacle: I didn't have any tools.

True: In a metal box under our bed, I had a modest selection of castoffs given to me by my dad, but this selection contained only two items that could have been identified as woodworking tools: a 16 oz. framing hammer and a battered handsaw with a rust-pitted blade. The others—wrenches and screwdrivers—had little application in a woodworking shop.

In short, woodworking was out of the question. I had no space and I had no tools. But I was young, and I didn't realize I was attempting something that couldn't be done.

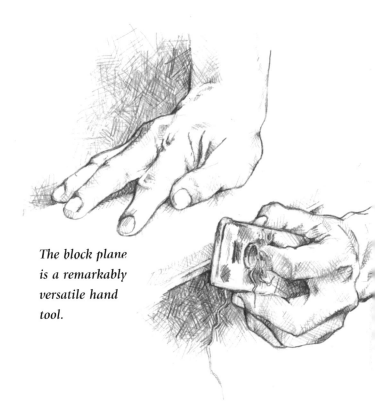

The block plane is a remarkably versatile hand tool.

MEXICAN CHESS SETS

We were living then in South Texas, just north of the Mexican border. On the weekends, we crossed the border into Reynosa or Matamoros to shop and to have dinner. Remarkably, although as a young school teacher making only $7200 a year I could do little in the way of impulse buying on the American side of the border, in Mexico prices were low enough so that I could actually shop.

Having been raised in the Midwest on a steady dict of manufactured goods, my wife and I were particularly taken by the handwork for sale in the Mexican markets: blouses and dresses decorated with needlework, casks and chests embellished with carving, simple chairs, and one of the staples of the Mexican border tourist shop: turned wooden chess sets.

On one of our trips across the border, I bought one of these chess sets. Then, after setting it up in our home, I took a close look at each of the pieces. Although obviously handmade—every turning was perceptibly different than every other—the execution of the pieces varied widely in quality. While several were sharply turned and cleanly sanded, others revealed bits of impacted bark or deep gouge marks. Others had cracked, as they dried.

True: It was handwork, but it wasn't good handwork. That was when I decided that my first woodworking project would be chess set.

A wooden-bodied spokeshave connects the contemporary woodworker to the centuries-old tradition of American woodworking.

A KNIFE, A COPING SAW, AND A SMALL MACHINIST'S VISE

I didn't have a lathe and couldn't afford to buy one. Too, I didn't know how to use one, so even if I'd had the money, probably I wouldn't have spent it. I decided then that my pieces would be carved. But with what tools?

In the bargain bin of a local lumberyard, I found a set of Japanese-made carving tools for a dollar. Seduced by the price and by the compartmentalized plastic roll in which the tools were packed, I bought them. Taking them home, I experimented on a piece of scrap white pine.

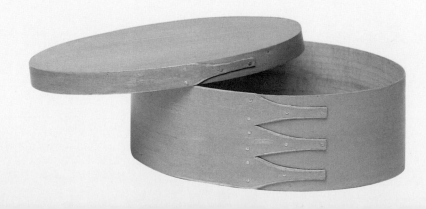

A metal-bodied spokeshave is a hybrid tool, having some of the characteristics of the plane and some of the characteristics of the classic wooden-bodied spokeshave.

I then went home to become a woodworker.

First, using the coping saw, I cut some white pine 1 x 2 to the length of the first chess piece I intended to make: the white queen. Then after an application of Elmer's household glue, I clamped two lengths of white pine together in my machinist's vise, thus creating the pine 2 x 2 I needed as my carving blank.

The next night, after work, I went outside into a light rain and clamped my vise to the angle-iron hitch at the front of our travel trailer and, with the coping saw, began to rough in the shape of the white queen. Then back inside, with a cookie sheet in my lap to catch the chips, I switched to my pocketknife and began to refine that rough shape.

At one dollar for a set of six, these tools were overpriced. Even though the Japanese are now noted for the quality of their edge tools, the metal in that particular set of carving tools wasn't any better than the metal in an auto ignition key. They wouldn't take an edge, they wouldn't have been able to hold it.

Frustrated, I returned to the lumber yard and selected a pocket knife and an oil stone, as well as a coping saw. Finally, at the last minute, I added a small machinist's vise.

Most areas could be excavated quite nicely with the pocket knife's primary blade, but I couldn't get that tool into some of the queen's tighter corners. Using the coarser side of my combination oil stone, I reworked that smaller blade into a very small and very sharp cutting tool, one perfectly suited to the cramped areas I wished to carve.

Later, as I carved my way through the chess set, I added other tools to my collection—several tiny rasps and files, a selection of sandpaper, a leather glove to protect the hand in which I held the work—and this turned out to be all I needed in the way of tooling for this project. True: A lathe would have been nice, and a new set of Swiss carving tools would have been fun to buy and fun to own, and the coping-saw work could have been more easily accomplished on a bandsaw. But I didn't have those things. So I did what I could with what I had, and in the process, I learned things about chess sets and carving and myself that I otherwise would not have known.

CHAPTER FOUR

▪MATERIALS▪

Beautiful woodwork requires beautiful wood. Bland, figureless material handicaps even the most accomplished craftsman. Unfortunately for the amateur woodworker, it isn't enough to buy material of a species known for its beauty. The woodworker must select only the most beautiful boards of that beautiful species.

Education is the first step in the acquisition of beautiful material. This is a process that probably should begin with a study of the grades assigned to hardwood lumber. True, small dealers with a limited selection often offer their material ungraded, as it came from the log. But larger dealers who carry a substantial inventory will offer it in grades, the best being FAS (First and Seconds) and the worst being No. 1 or No. 2 Common.

The top grade, FAS, will feature lumber that is essentially clear and free of defects on both sides. Selects, the next grade, is very much like FAS, with one exception: The lumber is essentially clear and defect-free on only its best side. This is an important consideration for the woodworker selecting lumber, which, in its finished state, will be seen from only one side; this is the case, for example, with the material used in the figured oak candlebox, *see* page 88. Below that grade, there are two common grades that might be carried by dealers in your area. No. 1 Common is the better of these grades and yet it will feature boards exhibiting a fairly generous measure of defects, which might include knots, pitch pockets, and wane. No. 2 Common is a bit worse than No. 1 Common, by definition containing an even more generous measure of defects.

These last two grades will be of limited use in a shop specializing in the construction of large pieces

Fancy Pails. Circa 1875–1885.
Attributed to Rufus Crosman (1848–1891) or
Daniel Boler (1804–1892),
Mt. Lebanon, New York.
(Larger) Red cedar, sumac, white pine, beech, iron.
6⅝ x 10x 9½ inches.
In ink: 1884 and illegible initials.

(Smaller) Red Cedar, sumac, white pine, fruitwood,
iron, copper-plated iron.
5⅛ x 6¾ x 9½ inches.
(From the collection of Hancock Shaker Village,
Pittsfield, Massachusetts.
Photo: Paul Rocheleau)

being suitable in such shops only for secondary applications, for example, hidden cleats. However, for the woodworker building small pieces—like those in this book—these grades might be worth consideration because, when working with small pieces, it's possible to cut around the defects. Many of the pieces appearing in this book were made from No. 1 cherry.

However, the woodworker's education can't be confined to grades, since there can be considerable variety of color and figure within the same grade.

It's also essential that the woodworker understand the variety of surfaces individual wood species can present. In large part, this education can only come through experience. It is necessary that a fair amount of lumber be purchased, handled, and used in the creation of wooden objects. It is necessary that some of this material be carried through the entire construction process, all the way from planing to sanding and finishing. It is necessary, too, that the woodworker live with certain photoreactive species—like cherry—some months or years after their use so that long-term changes in color can be observed.

But the initial steps in that education can be taken in galleries and shows by observing finished work. Libraries, too, can be important aides in the process since nearly all will have a least a single volume showing sharp color photography of finished wood samples in a variety of species. In addi-

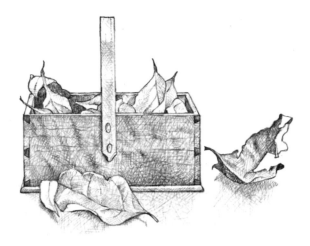

tion, there are a number of woodworking groups scattered across the country that count education among their goals, and these groups can be excellent sources for the amateur woodworker.

BUILDERS' SUPPLIERS

You can still buy hardwood at some companies whose primary function is to meet the needs of homebuilders. However, you are likely to find the price of the hardwood bought at such outlets to be quite high and the selection quite small, simply because most builders have little need for the kind of material used in the making of furniture and woodenware.

COMMERCIAL SUPPLIERS

Although commercial suppliers, like builders' suppliers, cater to the needs of the construction trades, these operations are likely to have quite extensive inventories of both native and tropical hardwoods. Much of that material will have been milled into hardwood flooring and trim intended for installation in expensive homes and in commercial locations. Luckily, the hardwood flooring company in my hometown always has several thousand feet of rough cherry, oak, and maple available for retail sales.

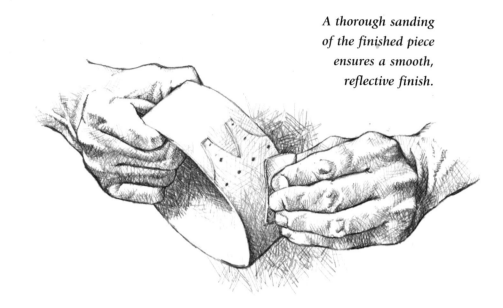

A thorough sanding of the finished piece ensures a smooth, reflective finish.

HOME IMPROVEMENT SUPPLIERS

Like the builders' suppliers, those businesses catering to the needs of the do-it-yourselfers (DIYers) is likely to have a small but expensive selection of certain kinds of native hardwoods. For the woodworker who has no access to the kind of tools required for material preparation—planer, tablesaw, and jointer—the material sold at home improvement suppliers can meet DIY needs better than other types of suppliers simply because the material they offer is often already, ripped, jointed, surfaced, and even resawn and planed to finished thicknesses other than ¾ inch.

STORES FOR THE WOODWORKING HOBBYIST

Because of their high prices, these stores might be seen as a last resort; however, I have visited them in order to pick up a small amount of a material I

Opposite: "Woodenware for the Workroom"
Two carrier projects.
(Smaller) Walnut and ash.
(Larger) Cherry and ash.

couldn't get any other way. For example, several years ago I was repairing a Windsor rocker built of mahogany. The notch at the bottom of one of the legs into which a rocker was set had broken out, splintering into many pieces, only some of which the owner had collected. Because I don't work with tropical woods, I had no pieces of mahogany which I could graft onto the damaged leg. I therefore made a trip to a store in my area which caters to hobbyists and bought a small block of mahogany with which I made the repair. True, I did pay several times the market price, but I was able to complete the job in a timely fashion.

MAIL-ORDER SUPPLIERS

Many of the stores that cater to the hobbyist also sell material and tools through mail-order catalogs. While this is the most convenient method of acquiring new material, there is a string attached: While the customer can specify species, grade, and size, the actual selection of boards is done by someone who has no knowledge of the specific requirements of the woodworker's project.

SAWMILLS

This is where the craftsman finds the best prices. It is also where the craftsman takes the greatest risks. While the sawyers in my area are skillful in the disciplines of tree felling and sawing logs into boards, most are less skillful in the area of lumber grading. Some, in fact, will hire outside contractors to come in and grade a batch of lumber before they ship that lumber to a customer.

In my area, I can buy fresh sawn cherry of a grade that approximates FAS for a couple of dollars a foot. This compares very favorably with the

ffive or more a foot commonly found at commercial suppliers and even more favorably with the ten or more a foot found at stores supplying the hobbyist.

However, the less expensive sawmill lumber does come with some strings attached. First, no sawmill I know will bother with really small lots. If you call and ask for ten board feet of 8/4 cherry, you may hear the sawmill operator laughing on the other end of the phone.

By joining together with other hobbyists it is possible to put together an order of sufficient size to interest a sawyer. Too, for the serious hobbyist, it may be worthwhile to buy, at one time, enough material for several years' worth of projects.

CUT YOUR OWN

I've made considerable use of this method, taking trees from my own woods, as well as taking nuisance trees from the land of friends and neighbors. On the plus side, this does permit the acquisition of very cheap material. In our area, I can have a man with a Wood-Mizer sawmill saw lumber for as little as twenty cents a board foot.

There are, however, reasons to avoid this method. First, it's a very labor-intensive method of material acquisition. In order to harvest your own lumber, it's necessary to clear an area large enough to accommodate the fallen tree. It is also necessary to undertake the considerable labor of felling the tree and the labor of bucking the tree into lengths suitable for the capacity of the sawmill. This method always generates a great deal of brush and firewood which must be cut up and carted off. And last, while this method sometimes produces beautiful material, it can also disappoint.

Several years ago, I took a number of trees from our woods, one of them a maple. This maple was especially important because I needed a supply of green maple for chair post stock. However, it was not until I had laid the maple on the ground, that I realized that what I had was not a length of usable trunk. Instead, I had a long, hollow tube of wood, the insides of which had rotted out years ago. Apparently, a hole in the tree's primary crotch—which was located maybe thirty feet off the ground—had allowed water to percolate down through the entire length of the trunk, rotting out all the usable wood and leaving behind only enough thickness to carry nourishment to the tree's limbs and leaves.

CHAPTER FIVE

▪ PROCESS ▪

*W*hen I first began to work with wood, I tended to work quickly, speeding from one operation to the next, allowing little time for planning and rehearsal. In the shop of a more experienced woodworker, such speed might have reflected skill and confidence, but in my shop that speed reflected the opposite conditions. I worked quickly because I wasn't sure I could successfully complete the projects begun. Would that set of dovetails come together properly? Would those tenons fit those mortises? Would pipe clamps bring that gapping glue joint together and would the glue then hold it tightly?

This uncertainty compelled me to work faster so that I could more quickly get the piece done and in that manner assure myself that I knew what I was doing.

I recognize the absurdity of this approach to shop processes-I think I recognized it even in those first years-but I was powerless to change the way in which I worked, and the truth is that, usually, this run-and-gun method got results. I did get work done, and it was generally done right. Maybe the finish had areas that didn't reflect enough light. Maybe a set of dovetails had a bit more gap than I wanted. But that finish would protect the table top from spilled drinks, and those dovetails would hold the drawer together.

Then gradually, over a period of years, as I acquired more confidence in my skills, I began to slow myself down, taking more time with each step, proceeding deliberately, rehearsing tricky processes before I attempted them.

GLUING UP

I started my rehearsals with the gluing up process.

In my shop, this is the operation that most demands my full attention. At any other point in the construction process, an unanticipated complication can, at worst, cause the loss of an individual

A sharp carving gouge quickly removes waste.

part, but during the gluing up process, an unanticipated complication can cause the loss of an entire piece. On more than one occasion, when drawing a glue-slathered joint together with pipe clamps, an unexpected bit of bad news has shifted me from tranquility to panic in a heartbeat.

Glue can be very unforgiving. This is particularly true of the white and yellow glues most of us use in our shops. Because of their relatively short open time (the amount of time available for the shifting of parts before the glue starts to grab), the gluing up process must proceed quickly enough so that it can be accomplished in the five to ten minute assembly windows these glues allow but still slowly enough so that parts can be adjusted into the optimum alignment.

If, in the middle of a glue-up, it becomes apparent that one of the joints is not going to come together in quite the right way, an immediate decision must be made: Can the joint be modified quickly enough to salvage this glue-up? Or should the piece be completely disassembled and the joints washed off so that fitting and regluing can take place at a more leisurely pace?

This is a decision I would prefer to make at my leisure, not impelled by the pressures of freshly glued joint components. For that 0I decided to begin rehearsing the gluing up process with dry joints, resolving any complications before reaching for the glue bottle.

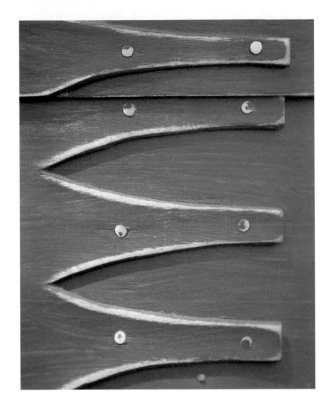

I begin rehearsals by clearing my bench of any tools and unneeded bits of wood. Next, I lay out the various parts of the piece about to be glued. At this point, I set the approximate clamping lengths on any pipe clamps or C-clamps. I then assemble the piece, bringing it partially together with the clamps.

It's important that mortise-and-tenon and dovetail joints not be fully seated when the joint components are dry. Yes, it is essential to determine that they are fit well enough so that moderate clamping pressure will bring them together (this is the reason for the partial assembly), but it is just as essential that complete seating of the joint components be delayed until the time of final assembly.

Pails.
(Left front pail) Circa 1850–1870.
Possibly Levi Stevens (1781–1867).
Canterbury or Enfield, New Hampshire.
White pine, maple, paint, iron, cloth, thread.
6 x 8¾ x 8 inches.

(Right front pail) Circa 1820–1850.
Probably New Lebanon, New York.
White pine, hickory, birch, stain, iron.
11¾ x 13½ inches.
(From the collection of Hancock Shaker Village, Pittsfield, Massachusetts. Photo: Paul Rocheleau)

There are two reasons for this delay. First, total seating of dry components may result in a set of joints fit so tightly that they can be separated only through the use of brute force (which can damage or destroy the parts). Second, glue acts as a lubricant, allowing parts that otherwise might stick (damaging or destroying the parts) to slide into the proper alignment.

Rehearsals may not eliminate every possible gluing-up complication, but they do reduce the odds of assembly-day catastrophe.

OTHER REHEARSALS

Eventually, I began to rehearse other tricky operations as well. If, for example, I'm about to run a long board over my jointer, first—with the jointer's switch in the off position—I hold the board in the correct infeed and outfeed alignments to determine whether there is enough room in my small shop. I perform similar rehearsals before running long or wide material over my tablesaw. I also rehearse any tricky tool grinding operations with the grinder's motor off, holding the tool next to the still wheel, estimating which positions will bring the tool and the wheel into the proper alignment. If I'm about to use a shaving tool on a complex contour or on a contour cut in a piece of wildly grained wood, I do a dry run, holding the cutting edge above the work, trying to get a sense of the hand positions needed to use and those areas that will require a reversal of the tool or the work in order to cut in the direction of rising grain.

In addition to physical rehearsals, I also take time to think my way through construction sequences, rehearsing procedures in my mind so that construction can proceed in a manner that permits operations to be done in the proper order. This is very important in the gluing up of sub-assemblies for a complicated construction.

Several years ago, when beginning to glue up the frame of a Hepplewhite huntboard, I glued the drawer rails and stiles together before attaching them to the front legs. This method would have worked out fine if both the upper and lower rails had attached to the legs with mortise-and-tenon joints. Unfortunately, only the lower rail had tenons. The upper rail attached to the legs with a

big, fat dovetail on either end, and those dovetails had to be squeezed into their mortises from the top down before the tenons in the lower rail could be seated into their mortises. I did eventually manage to get the pieces together—with considerable effort and even more frustration. I learned quickly that the process would have been much simpler if I had left off that top rail until after the lower rail (and the attached short rails and stiles) had been first installed into the legs.

CHAPTER SIX

▪ SHAKER ▪ PRODUCTION RUN

MAKING MANY AS "ONE OF A KIND"

It's much more efficient to make ten copies of the same piece than it is to make one copy of ten different pieces, and this efficiency is the primary appeal of the production run. A series of candleboxes is presented here showing how the woodworker can give some consideration to the introduction of one-of-a-kind characteristics by making use of strategies that allow variation in the items being made during that production run.

A woodworker who sets up his booth at a craft show with every item exactly like the other may soon find that potential customers glance at the work and walk away, disenchanted by the sameness. And this disenchantment may occur regardless of the artistry and skill evident in the work. Similarly, if a woodworker makes his relatives a dozen identical Christmas gifts, on Christmas morning after the packaging has been collected and discarded, and after everybody has had a chance to look at everybody else's gifts, the sameness of the gifts may diminish their apparent value.

INTRODUCING ONE-OF-A-KIND CHARACTERISTICS

The main advantage of the production run is the efficiency in making many copies of the same piece. Whether the items will be gifts or for sale, the woodworker will add pleasure and value for the recipients—as well as increased satisfaction for himself—by introducing one-of-a-kind characteristics into the items being made in that production run.

The idea of variation may appeal to the woodworker, but he may be left wondering what kind of strategies he should consider introducing into his production run. The series of candleboxes presented here makes use of production run methods that will allow the use of three such strategies.

Materials

The first and most obvious way to differentiate among the items in a production run is to vary the materials from which those items are made. This can be done in two ways. First and most simply, different items in the run can be made of different

The wood for this box—a mix of cherry and walnut—reveals the presence of several knotholes.

materials. The craftsman can make the first from walnut, the second from maple, the third from cherry, and so on. Second—and I think this presents more intriguing aesthetic possibilities— the craftsman can experiment with different combinations of materials, including two or more species in the same piece. In the case of the candleboxes presented here, I used both methods.

Two of the boxes are made entirely of white pine, and another—with the exception of the small walnut pull that is attached—is made entirely of cherry. The remaining boxes are mixtures of woods: a cherry box with knotholes is finished with a walnut lid, also containing a knothole; a walnut box is finished with a curly maple top, as is another cherry box.

I'm planing a bevel on the lid of one of the partially assembled boxes shown.

Although this method does allow the woodworker to make better use of each machine set-up, it is not quite as simple a process as making an entire series of items from the same material. You will find that a bit of additional planning is required.

For example, if a production run is to include one piece made of cherry, it is essential that the craftsman thickness a sufficient amount of cherry to make all the parts for that one piece because if, during the assembly process, the crafts-man discovers that he doesn't have enough cherry of the proper thickness to make all necessary parts, the production process grinds to a halt while cherry is found, thicknessed, ripped to width, and cut to length. This kind of time penalty can eat into any efficiency gains made through the use of production-run methods.

My solution to this problem is to thickness-plane more material of any one species than I will need for a particular item in the production run. This method not only ensures sufficient material of each necessary species, it also offers one other advantage: choice.

Sometimes a length of material that looked very promising in the rough is much less promising after it has been surfaced. In the case of this particular production run, for example, I pulled out a number of short walnut boards, only to discover after planing that several were marred by odd, tarry streaks that ran too deep to be removed by my planer. Because I had thicknessed more than enough walnut, I didn't have to locate new material, reset my planer at one inch, and once again work my way down to ½ inch.

Also, thicknessing more material than an item actually requires offers some insurance against

A combination of heartwood and sapwood is also used in making the lid of this cherry box.

the woodworker's mistakes, especially against the the board that's cut a half-inch too short or that was mistakenly edge-jointed against the grain.

True: This approach does mean that when you're done with a production run, you might have a bit more ½-inch-thick walnut than you needed, but I've found that if I set that ½-inch material aside, eventually it will fit in somewhere.

Pull Design

The nature of the piece being produced can sometimes dictate the kinds of differentiation a craftsman might employ. For example, in the case of this particular candlebox, it seemed to me that the pull was one element that could be used as a vehicle for the introduction of variety.

In the case of the Shaker candlebox on which these variations are loosely based, the pull was a shallow half-circle carved into the lid. In fact, this is a pull I used in making the walnut box with the curly maple top. However, every other pull is different than that found on the original. Two others—those on the pine boxes—are also carved into the surfaces of the lids, but the shape of each is more involved than the carved half-circle of the Shaker original. Two other pulls are carved from contrasting wood and then set into notches cut into the lids. In the case of the tiny walnut pull on top of the cherry box, the walnut simply stands above the surface of the box. In the case of the cherry pull that is set into the curly maple top, however, the pull also extends down over the edge and reaches about ¾ of an inch over the box's end panel.

The last pull is simply a finger-sized knothole. Although a found rather than manufactured shape, this was the most difficult of the pulls to produce, simply because of the difficulty of finding a walnut board of sufficient width with a knothole in just the right place.

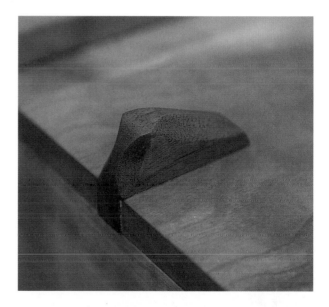

The cherry box has a small walnut pull.
Because white pine is easily worked with edge tools,
I use it for the two boxes with carved pulls.

Dovetail Patterns

Because I cut my dovetails by hand, this is a method of differentiation that fits particularly well into my shop routine. If one item in a production run is laid out with five tails on a side, the next item might be laid out with seven tails or four tails on that same side. Also, in addition to varying the number of tails on an end, I like to experiment with different arrangements of those tails. Conventional joinery uses tails of approximately equal size across the width of a board. This approach can be an effective way of introducing visual rhythm to that union of side and end. But there are other possibilities.

As I did when constructing several of these candleboxes, the tails can be broken up into different patterns, in which tails of unequal size are employed on the same end of the piece. For example, a craftsman might have fairly wide tails at the top and bottom of a side, while clustering several smaller tails in the middle. This strategy and several variations of it were used in the joinery of the candleboxes.

I've also experimented with different arrangements of tails on the different ends of the same box. This is a strategy that works remarkably well with this series of candleboxes because the shorter end over which the lid will slide already dictates a different arrangement of tails and pins than can be used on the other end of the box.

The dovetails on the right-hand box have been glued. The dovetails of the left-hand box have been dry-fit. Notice that the dry-fit dovetails have not been fully seated. In order to prevent the sides from splitting, I bring the joints completely together only after they have been lubricated with glue. The joints are then squeezed together with a set of pipe clamps.

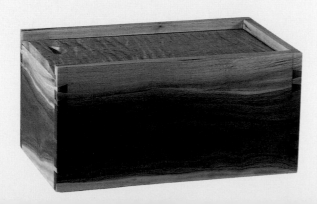

Recently, I've been making use of walnut in which there is a combination of heartwood and sapwood.

The grooves into which the edges of the the box bottom are fit are plugged after the box has been assembled.

Differentiation

It is possible to produce objects with a one-of-a-kind feel while making use of production-run methods. All it takes is a bit of head-scratching to develop a set of differentiation strategies suitable for the items being made.

Building the Candlebox

I began by planing my material to the ½-inch thickness that the boxes require, running a bit extra of each species to allow for defective material as well as errors in craftsmanship. I next ripped out the sides and ends and plowed the grooves in which the bottom is housed, as well as the grooves in which the top slides. It would be possible to cut stopped-grooves and thereby eliminate the plugs that fill the through-grooves I used on these boxes; however, that's a much more time-consuming procedure, and I must admit that I don't find anything unsightly about the plugs. In fact, I think they add another element of visual interest to the boxes' joinery.

Materials List*

Part	Quantity	Dimensions
Side	2 pcs.	½ x 7 x 14
Tall end	1 pc.	½ x 7 x 8½
Short end	1 pc.	½ x 6 x 8½
Bottom	1 pc.	½ x 8 x 13½
Top	1 pc.	½ x 8 x 13¾
Plug	4 pcs.	¼ x ¼ x ⅜ shaved to fit

* These are net measurements. Surplus should be added to dovetailed parts to allow them to be planed or sanded flush.

I then cut these sides and ends to length.

Next, I turned my attention to the lids and bottoms. The bottoms have bevels planed on all four sides to fit into the grooves cut into the inside surfaces of the boxes' sides and ends. The tops have bevels planed on both sides and one end. I chose to cut these bevels with hand planes.

I then cut the dovetails on all of the boxes. This is another particular operation that I perform by hand for very personal reasons: I like a quiet shop, and enjoy the opportunity to make use of my physical skills.

Then I scraped and sanded all pieces and assemble the boxes around the bottoms.

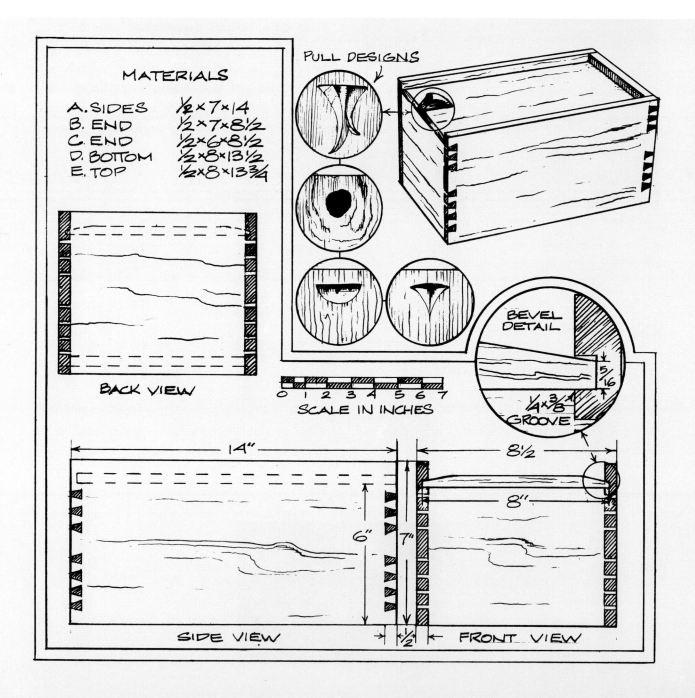

MATERIALS

A. SIDES   ½×7×14
B. END   ½×7×8½
C. END   ½×6×8½
D. BOTTOM   ½×8×13½
E. TOP   ½×8×13¾

PULL DESIGNS

BACK VIEW

SCALE IN INCHES
0 1 2 3 4 5 6 7

BEVEL DETAIL

5/16
¼×3/8 GROOVE

14"

8½"

8"

6"

7"

½

SIDE VIEW   FRONT VIEW

IN THE SHAKER
▪MANNER▪

CHARLES HARVEY

*E*ven today, years after the golden age of Shaker woodenware, contemporary craftsmen continue to reproduce the distinctive forms created by nineteenth-century Shaker woodworkers. Charles Harvey, one such contemporary craftsman, is the subject of the following profile.

Charles Harvey, of Berea, Kentucky, is a natural.

With his improbable mustache, his metal-framed glasses, and his strong and confident hands, he evokes the craftsmen of an earlier and—at least in our imaginations—simpler time. Like the Shaker reproductions he builds, he is lean, without superfluous weight. In his clean, well-ordered shop, he moves with purpose but without haste, each motion choreographed to make the most efficient use of time and effort. Rocking in the showroom of his shop in a chair he built with his own hands, surrounded by the sturdy Shaker boxes, chairs, and casework he offers for sale, Charles is comfortable and at ease. This is where he belongs. The aesthetics of the Shakers—the simplicity, the efficiency, the honest reliability—have not been forcibly grafted onto his work. These qualities are simply extensions of his personality.

A SIMPLE LIFE OF SELF-SUFFICIENCY

Many woodworkers make their first contact with the United Society of Believers in Christ's Second Coming (the Shakers) because of interest in their furniture and woodenware. Some, perhaps seeing simple as synonymous with easily built, are looking for shortcuts to craftsmanship. Others find an expression of their own personal aesthetic in the clean plainness of Shaker woodwork. Still others are fascinated by the Shakers' two-hundred-year experiment in the creation of a utopian society based on a rigidly defined Christianity.

Harvey's first contact with the Shakers put him in this last group.

In the nineteen-sixties, at the recommendation of a high school English teacher, Charles read Henry David Thoreau's *Walden*, an event that encouraged him to examine alternative lifestyles. Later the magazine *Mother Earth News* and the back-to-the-land movement of the seventies, together with a lifelong interest in spirituality, inspired in Charles an interest in utopian societies, particularly those with a strong religious bent. And it was in this context that he made his initial discovery of the Shakers. "It was first about their society," he explains, "because at that time I wasn't a woodworker."

In fact, a number of years would pass before he would approach the Shakers from a woodworking perspective.

In 1978, Charles had a job exercising thoroughbred horses in the Chicago, Illinois, area. While on vacation from this job, he stopped in Berea, Kentucky, and there met Warren May, a professional woodworker specializing in dulcimers. "I bought a dulcimer from Warren," Charles recalls. "Then, on the way home, I thought: Wouldn't it be great if I could move to Berea and work for Warren May?"

Shortly after this visit, motivated by financial considerations, he left his job exercising thoroughbreds and began working in construction. "Then I got laid off in 1980 when the construc-

tion business in Chicago had some hard times, so I packed up my stuff and drove to Berea in my Volkswagen Camp Mobile and reintroduced myself to Warren. He hired me that same afternoon."

For a year and a half, Charles worked for Warren May in what amounted to an informal apprenticeship, during which he learned woodworking fundamentals and developed skills and confidence. He then decided to go out on his own, so he bought a Shopsmith, a Sears band saw, and prepared to do business in an old freight warehouse.

"I did everything," he says with pride. "I built dulcimers. I did three kitchens, probably the only kitchens in Berea with handcut dovetails on the drawers. I had no idea how to bring a job in at a specific cost, because I was in such a passion about the woodwork. I just wanted the work to be the best I could make it."

Opposite: Charles Harvey's workshop is filled with his collection of antique tools— many of which see daily use in his shop.

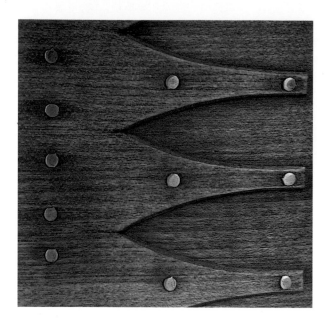

Then, on a trip to the restored Shaker community at Pleasant Hill, Kentucky, Charles rediscovered the Shakers, this time as a woodworker; and the furniture and woodenware he saw there resonated with his not-yet-articulated aesthetic. "When I was working for Warren, he was doing fancy period stuff. But I'm a simple person, and when I saw the Shaker stuff, it just looked right. it's honest, carefully constructed. It doesn't leave a lot of room for fudging. You can't hide things or balance things out with moldings. All the grace that a Shaker piece has is contained in its fundamental elements."

SHAKER FURNITURE- AND BOX-MAKING

After declaring himself a builder of Shaker furniture, Charles took samples of his work to Pleasant Hill and showed it to the people in the gift shop, hoping to generate some business. "They liked my work, but they had a contract with a company to produce their furniture so they turned me down." But the shopkeeper said: "Charles, do you realize no one in Kentucky is building Shaker boxes?"

"So," says Charles, "I went to the curator and got permission to take rubbings from the original boxes, and from those rubbings I made a set of patterns and forms."

Although he had accurate patterns, he found that there was little information available about the methods the Shakers used to produce their boxes: "At that time, there was nothing in print about how to make these boxes, and the last Shaker brother who made them died in 1961. And I'm not aware of anyone who's unearthed a journal explaining exactly how a Shaker made a box."

Because of this lack of information, Charles' methods evolved through a combination of trial and error and a careful examination of museum collections of boxes and box-making equipment. "Probably the best belongs to the Shaker museum at Old Chatham in New York."

"After I saw their stuff pictured in Shea's book, I drove up to Old Chatham and said: 'I'm Charles Harvey. I'm the oval boxmaker for Pleasant Hill. Where's this oval box display?'"

"And the woman at the desk said: 'That's been down for years.'

"I must have showed my disappointment, because she called the curator, and she took me back into cold storage and let me make patterns from the Shakers' bending forms."

Over the last decade, as a result of his study of museum collections and the experience he's gained from the construction of several thousand boxes, Charles has moved from the production of boxes with plain-sawn maple sides and plywood tops and bottoms, to the production of boxes with quarter-sawn maple sides and white pine tops and bottoms. This makes his boxes very faithful to the originals on display in museums—so faithful, in fact, that Charles' boxes have been sold in the gift shops of Shaker museums across the United States and in almost every country in the Western World.

Box-making is the key to Charles business. Although he also sells a selection of Shaker chair and casework reproductions, it is the box-making portion of his business that usually serves as the first point of contact with customers, initiating a relationship that may last for years as customers assemble a complete set of nine nested boxes or as they move from boxes to chairs and casework. "The Shaker box is a familiar icon," says Charles.

"When you hold it in your hand, you know you're holding a well-crafted item. It has presence. It speaks of the Shaker ethic.

Just some of Charles Harvey's wide variety of oval boxes and carriers.

"Some people come into my shop and buy one box, and then it becomes their manifest destiny to have all nine. I even have some customers who have assembled entire nests of nine for two or three family members, in addition to the nest they assembled for themselves."

Many visitors purchase a box, but want to add to their collections later; so Charles has entered the mail-order business, sending out an annual brochure to people all over the country. Although they are much more expensive to ship, his chairs too have been sent all over the country. These typically go to customers who have first visited his shop in Berea and have taken the time to examine the chairs, sit in them and find the size that best suits their bodies.

Charles also makes many sales in the showroom that adjoins his workroom. One of the advantages to working in Berea is the steady flow of foot traffic drawn to the town by its growing national reputation for high-quality craft work.

Over the years, Charles has become adept at dealing with browsing customers as he works at his bench. He has learned how to answer their questions about Shaker life and society, how to explain various shop procedures, how to build a relationship that might turn into a sale—all without losing track of the work his hands are doing.

SIMPLICITY RATHER THAN STATUS

"Period furniture—Queen Anne, Chippendale, Federal—was built to show the owner's status," he explains. "The people who originally owned it would have had expensive cars, if they'd been available. Their furniture reflected their place in life."

This, according to Charles Harvey, represents the essential difference between period and Shaker furniture. The carving, the elaborate turning, the veneering—all the things that give period furniture its surface appeal—were intended to say to visitors in the home: "I have the kind of wealth it takes to possess work requiring so many man-hours of labor". Shaker furniture, on the other hand, lacks this elaborate surface manipulation, relying instead on the graceful interplay of its structural parts for its beauty, and it is this directness and simplicity that energize Charles in his daily pursuit of perfection in the building Shaker reproductions.

Charles Harvey rocks in the showroom of his shop in Berea, Kentucky. Behind him some of his chairs hang, *Shaker style, from pegs. Four pyramids of oval boxes can be seen atop a row of Shaker benches.*

WOODENWARE FOR
▪THE KITCHEN▪

For much of the country, the middle years of the nineteenth century marked a transition from the widespread use of handmade household goods to the widespread use of manufactured household goods.

The originals on which the following reproductions are based were all handmade and were all likely to have seen use in the kitchen.

WALNUT SCOOP

I couldn't find any source that identified the use the Shakers made of this particular scoop, which appears in Ejner Handberg's *Shop Drawings of Shaker Furniture and Woodenware*. With its large capacity, it might have been employed in an agricultural setting to scoop animal feed into the troughs of chickens or pigs.

I chose, however, to see it as a piece of kitchenware. There, it might have been used to scoop flour or beans or sugar from a large storage container.

Materials List

A. Scoop   1 pc.   3¹⁄₁₆ x 8 x 21¹¹⁄₁₆

Construction

This scoop is probably the most demanding construction in this book, requiring nearly two full days of shop time.

I began by band-sawing the outside profile of the scoop from a block of four-inch thick walnut. I then moved to the drill press, where, using a 1-inch Forstner bit, I crumbed out the scoop's large central depression. To accomplish this, I set the drill press to drill to three different depths, the greatest depth being used to clean out that part of the depression closest to the handle (where it is deepest), and the shallowest depth being used to clean out that part of the depression closest to the lip.

After cleaning out the scoop's depression, I then bored a row of one-inch holes through the handle with the block standing on edge. These holes were then refined with carving gouges and a rasp to form an opening for the user's fingers.

Since my band saw couldn't handle the eight-inch width of the scoop stood on edge, I used a bow saw to rough in the side profile—a task made easier since I had already removed material from the central depression.

The four-inch-thick blank of walnut has been sawn to the scoop's outside profile.

The bow saw permits me to cut material that is too wide for my band saw.

Gouges are used to fair the scoop's inside surfaces.

Then, with a wide-sweep carving gouge, I defined that central depression, later cleaning up those tool marks with a smaller gouge, followed by rasps, a flexible steel scraper, and sandpaper.

The convex surfaces on the outside of the scoop were much easier to form. These I shaped with a drawknife and spokeshave, removing the material very rapidly.

The drawknife in the foreground (left) is used to rough in the scoop's outside shape. The shape is then refined by a spokeshave as shown. Further work is done with a flexible metal scraper and sandpaper.

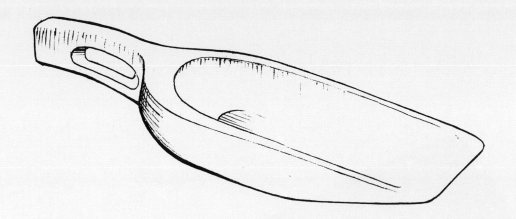

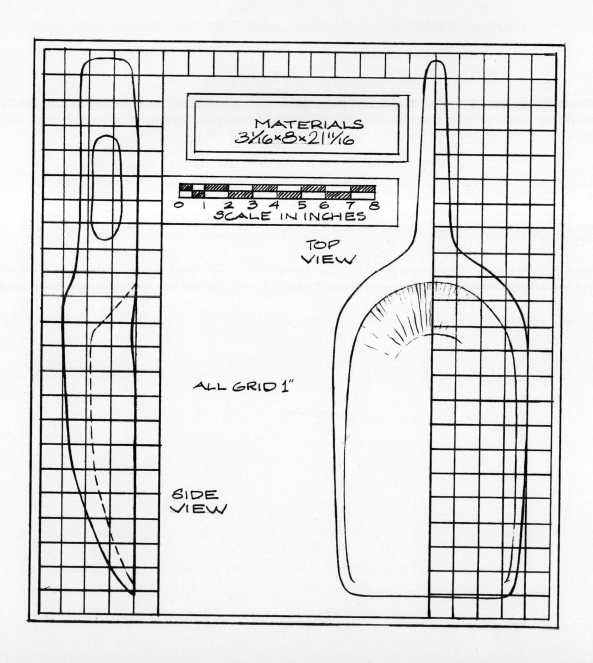

MATERIALS
3/16×8×21 1/16

0 1 2 3 4 5 6 7 8
SCALE IN INCHES

TOP
VIEW

ALL GRID 1"

SIDE
VIEW

SASSAFRAS PADDLE

Patterned after one appearing in in June Sprigg and Jim Johnson's *Shaker Woodenware: A Field Guide,* Volume 2, this simple piece can be made in less than an hour, but it is, nevertheless, an object that can prove useful in the kitchen as an aide in mixing ingredients.

The original was purchased from the Shakers at the Canterbury community in 1953.

Materials List
A. Paddle   1 pc.   ½ x 2½ x 12 7/16

Construction
After selecting clear and straight-grained stock of an appropriate species, I cut the paddle's profile on the band saw.

Then, blocking the paddle into place on my bench top with four stops, I began to plane the taper that runs across the full width of the piece, from its greatest thickness at the top of the handle to its least thickness at the tip of the blade.

After clamping a piece of scrap plywood to my bench, I enclose the paddle with four tacked stops.

Then, with a jack plane, I begin to plane the taper, making many passes on the stock nearest the blade's tip and few passes on the stock nearest the top of the handle.

Notice the pencil line on the edge of the paddle blank. That line shows the piece's finished thickness.

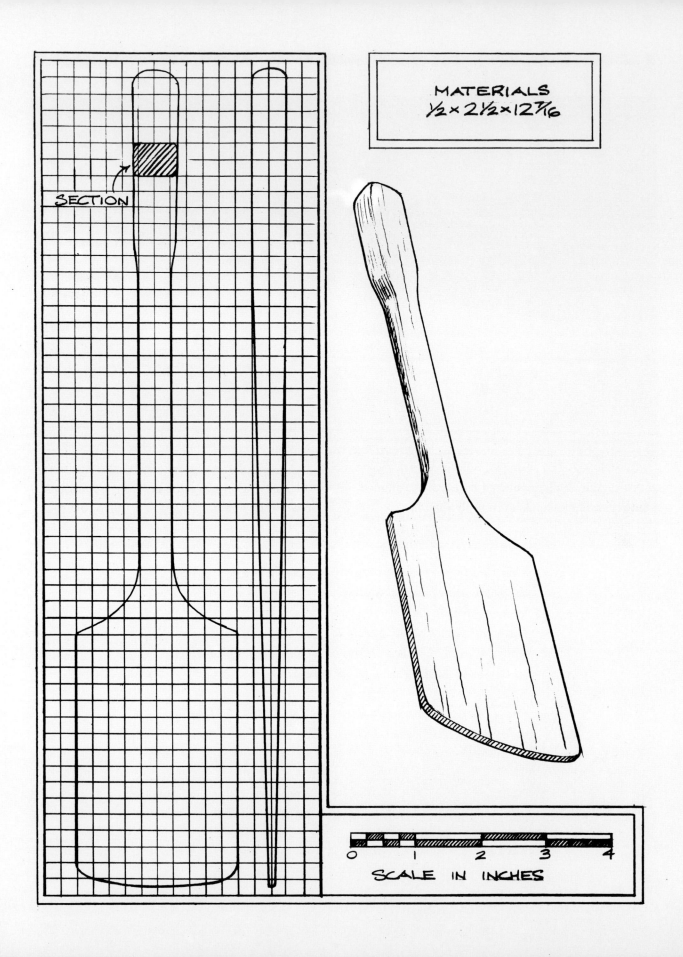

SECTION

MATERIALS
½ × 2½ × 12⁷⁄₁₆

SCALE IN INCHES

0   1   2   3   4

WALNUT DIPPER

One of a number of dippers pictured in my sources, this example is distinguished by a puffy, rounded contour, which extends even to the handle.

Materials List

A. Dipper   1 pc.   4$\frac{1}{16}$ x 4$\frac{7}{8}$ x 7$\frac{3}{16}$

Construction

I'd be interested in knowing more about how the Shakers actually made these little dippers. The process must reconcile the need to grip the work securely enough so that it can be shaped with carving tools with the need to grip the work gently enough so that the dipper's relatively weak side walls are not deformed.

I started by roughing in the dipper's interior using a Forstner bit in the drill press in much the same way as I formed the central depression in the scoop (*see* page 60). I then went back and undercut the side walls with a wide-sweep gouge.

On the band saw, I next cut the dipper's round profile, leaving in place the material from which I would cut the handle. Then, laying this squat cylinder on its side, I roughed in the handle with the band saw. This operation is a little tricky because it must be done with the area being sawn—the handle—unsupported by the band-saw table. If you're uncomfortable with this approach, I would suggest that a coping saw be used here.

Next, I began to shape the dipper's exterior with my gouge. To hold the work securely without damaging its side walls, I did two things. First, I snugged the jaws of my vise against the side walls, as shown in the photos. I then used a Quick-Grip clamp to pin the work against the screw on my vise. While working on the lower half of the dipper, I snugged the clamp pad against the dipper's flat bottom surface. When I worked on the upper half of the dipper, I put a waste block inside the dipper's body and snugged the clamp pad against that waste block. In this manner, I was able to hold the dipper while I worked it with carving gouges.

After crumbing out the waste at the drill press, I define the interior side walls with a carving gouge.

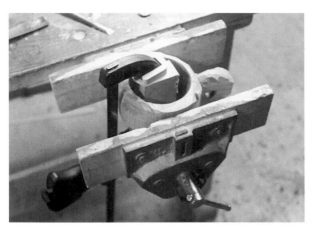

This photo shows the pad of the Quick-Grip clamp pressing a waste block against the bottom of the dipper.

This method of securing the work permits me to shape the walnut stock with carving gouges.

MATERIALS
$4\frac{1}{16} \times 4\frac{7}{8} \times 7\frac{3}{16}$

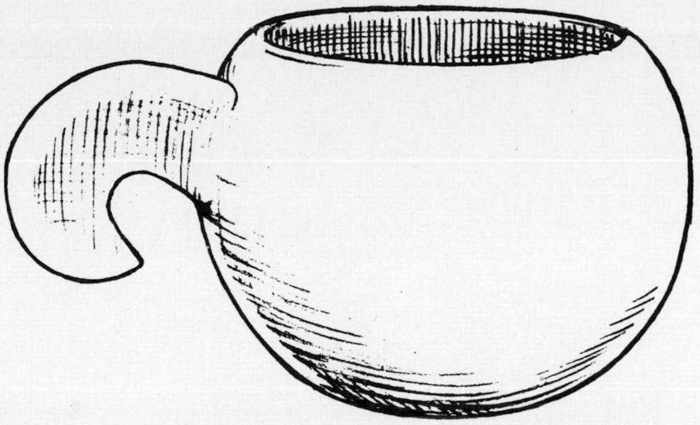

¼ GRID?

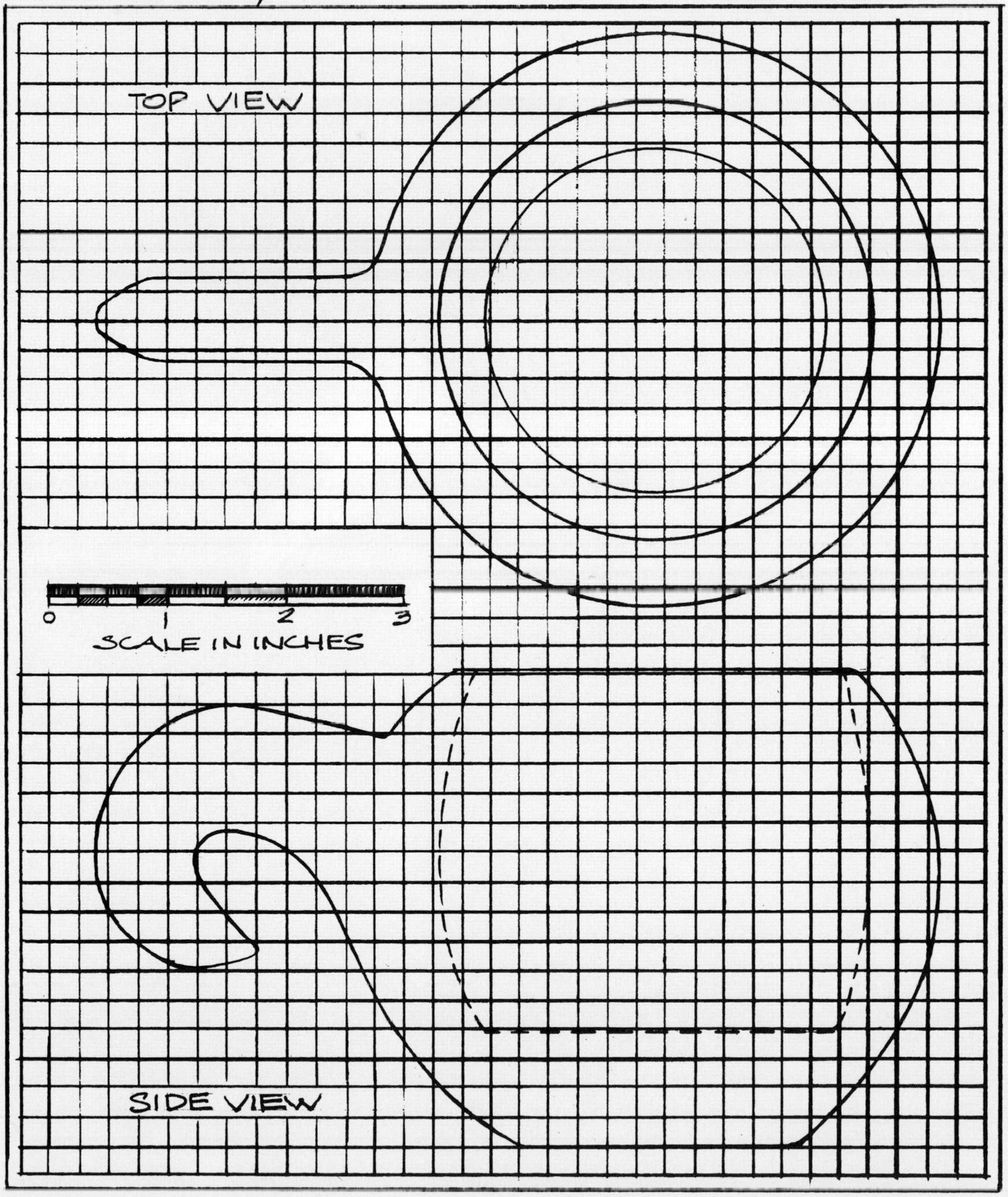

TOP VIEW

SCALE IN INCHES
0   1   2   3

SIDE VIEW

CURLY MAPLE
SERVING TRAY

According to Ejner Handberg, the original of this tray was made of pine, and I think that would have been, structurally at least, a perfectly satisfactory material for this particular piece. I chose, however, to make mine from some heavily figured curly maple for purely aesthetic reasons.

Materials List

A. Sides   2 pcs. $7/16$ x $4\frac{3}{8}$ x $17\frac{15}{16}$

B. Ends   2 pcs. $\frac{1}{2}$ x $5\frac{3}{16}$ x 11

C. Bottom   1 pc. $7/16$ x $10\frac{1}{8}$ x $17\frac{15}{16}$

D. Nails

Construction

After thicknessing the material, and after ripping it to width and cutting it to length, I dovetailed the sides and ends together.

This process is not as intimidating as it may, at first, appear, and there are many books which detail the necessary steps.

The bottom is then nailed into place.

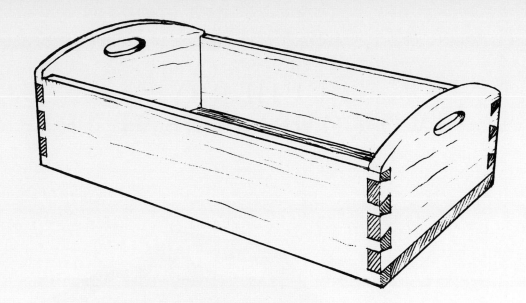

½ GRID

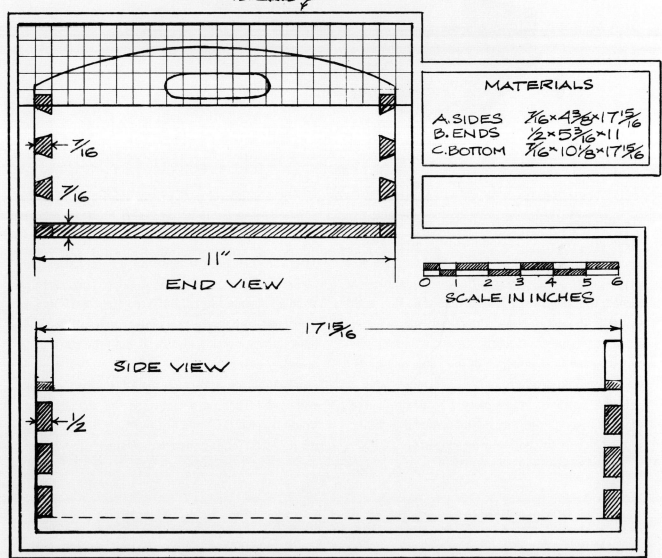

MATERIALS

A. SIDES	$\frac{7}{16} \times 4\frac{3}{8} \times 17\frac{15}{16}$	
B. ENDS	$\frac{1}{2} \times 5\frac{3}{16} \times 11$	
C. BOTTOM	$\frac{7}{16} \times 10\frac{1}{8} \times 17\frac{15}{16}$	

$\frac{7}{16}$

$\frac{7}{16}$

11"

END VIEW

0 1 2 3 4 5 6

SCALE IN INCHES

$17\frac{15}{16}$

SIDE VIEW

½

CHERRY
TWO-COMPARTMENT TRAY

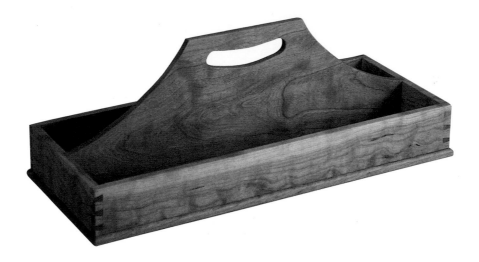

The original of this tray, also drawn by Ejner Handberg, while simple and featuring an elegantly contoured divider, was not assembled with a similarly elegant joinery. Instead of dovetails at each corner, the sides were fastened to the ends with nailed butt joints. The divider, too, was held in place with nailed butt joints. Also, the bottom was nailed to the bottom edges of the sides and ends, then planed flush all around.

Before assembling this piece, I decided to make some changes in the way it was fastened together and in the way the bottom was shaped.

Construction

After thicknessing the material, I band-sawed the two sweeping curves on the divider. Then, with a ¾-inch Forstner bit, I defined the ends of the finger hole, connecting these two ends with a saber saw. I then shaved, rasped, and sanded all the sawn surfaces.

I next ripped and cut to length the tray's sides and ends. Then, after cutting the dadoes that would receive the ends of the tray's divider, I cut the dovetails joining the tray's frame.

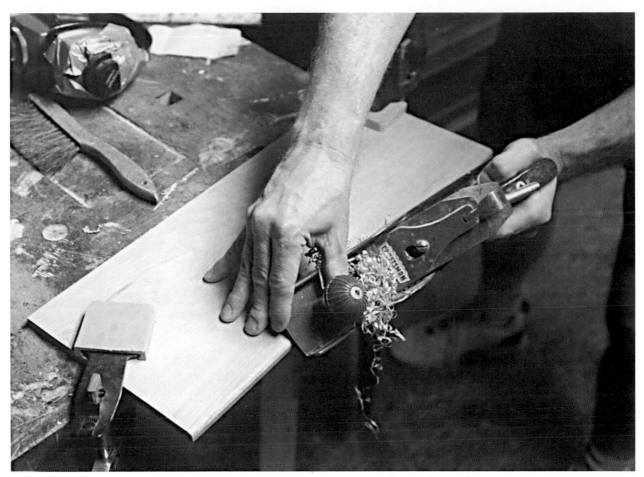

Clamping the tray bottom to my bench top, I round the edge with many passes of my jack plane.

I slid the divider into place, securing it with glue and a half dozen small nails.

Although the bottom of the Shaker original was planed flush all around, I decided to cut it ⅛ inch oversize on all four sides and then shape that excess into a quarter round with a jack plane. I then nailed the bottom into place.

Materials List

A.	Sides	2 pcs.	⅜ x 2¼ x 18⅝
B.	Ends	2 pcs.	⅜ x 2¼ x 7⁵⁄₁₆
C.	Bottom	1 pc.	⅜ x 7⁹⁄₁₆ x 18⅞
D.	Divider	1 pc.	⁵⁄₁₆ x 6½ x 18⅛
E.	Nails		

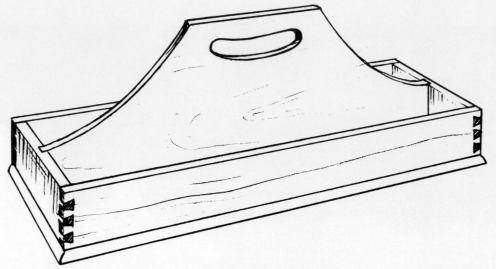

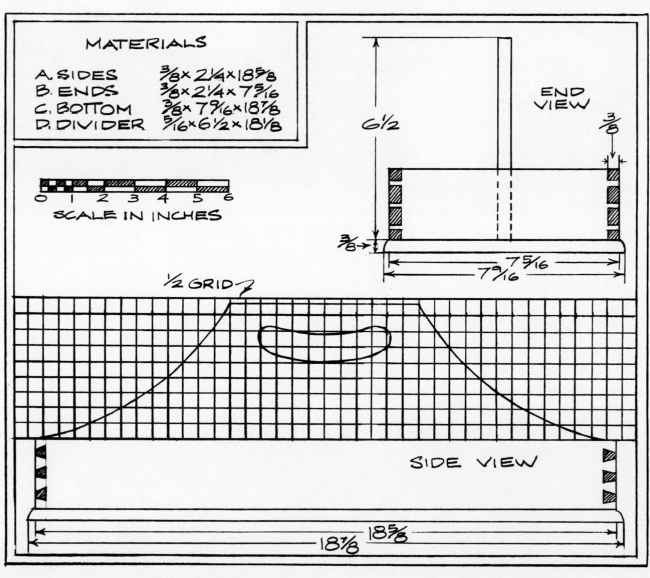

MATERIALS

A. SIDES $\frac{3}{8} \times 2\frac{1}{4} \times 18\frac{5}{8}$
B. ENDS $\frac{3}{8} \times 2\frac{1}{4} \times 7\frac{5}{16}$
C. BOTTOM $\frac{3}{8} \times 7\frac{9}{16} \times 18\frac{7}{8}$
D. DIVIDER $\frac{5}{16} \times 6\frac{1}{2} \times 18\frac{1}{8}$

0 1 2 3 4 5 6
SCALE IN INCHES

$\frac{1}{2}$ GRID

END VIEW

$6\frac{1}{2}$

$\frac{3}{8}$

$\frac{3}{8}$

$7\frac{5}{16}$

$7\frac{9}{16}$

SIDE VIEW

$18\frac{7}{8}$

$18\frac{5}{8}$

The cherry two-compartment tray is shown here with the walnut and ash carrier from the project section "Woodenware for the Workroom."

WOODENWARE FOR
▪THE SEWING ROOM▪

*A*ll of the items reproduced in the following section—a set of sewing steps, a spool holder, and three clothes hangers—were all made to be used by Shaker Sisters in their sewing rooms.

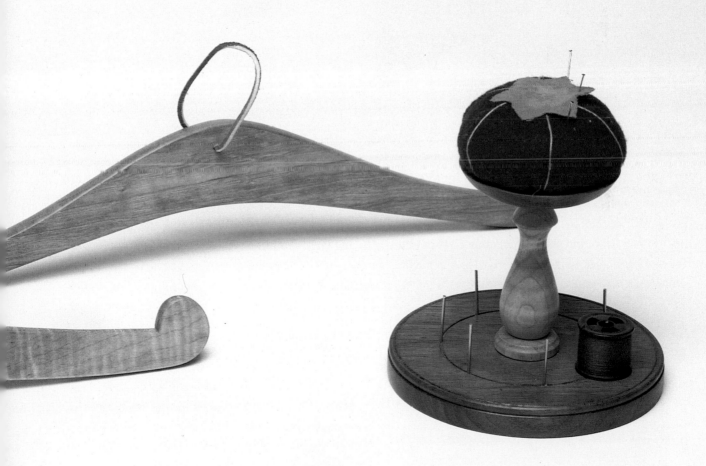

SEWING STEPS

These are very attractive steps. They are not, however, very well engineered. As I noted in my Introduction, during my work on this book these steps were knocked from a temporary bench I'd set up in my shop. They fell to the floor, partially separating the top step from the sides. If a better style of joinery had been used in their construction, the partial separation would not have occurred.

Materials List

A. Sides   2 pcs. $\frac{5}{16}$ x $7\frac{15}{16}$ x 8

B. Top step   1 pc. $\frac{5}{16}$ x $4\frac{1}{4}$ x $8\frac{1}{2}$

C. Bottom step   1 pc. $\frac{5}{16}$ x $4\frac{3}{8}$ x $8\frac{1}{2}$

D. Brace   1 pc. $\frac{5}{16}$ x $3\frac{7}{8}$ x $7\frac{1}{8}$

E. Nails

Construction

For these steps, I selected a length of cherry showing both a slightly wavy figure and what I saw as a very handsome mix of heartwood and sapwood on each edge. Then, for the steps themselves, I chose two pieces showing mostly heartwood with a thin band of sapwood along the front edge. The arched brace was made from a length of heartwood.

After planing the material to the proper thickness, I ripped the parts to width and cut them to length. I then band-sawed the arch in the brace.

Next, I set up the dado head on my table saw and cut the stopped grooves on the inside face of the sides into which the brace is set, finishing these grooves with a chisel. I then cut the two dadoes on the underside of the top step.

Finally, I nailed the steps together.

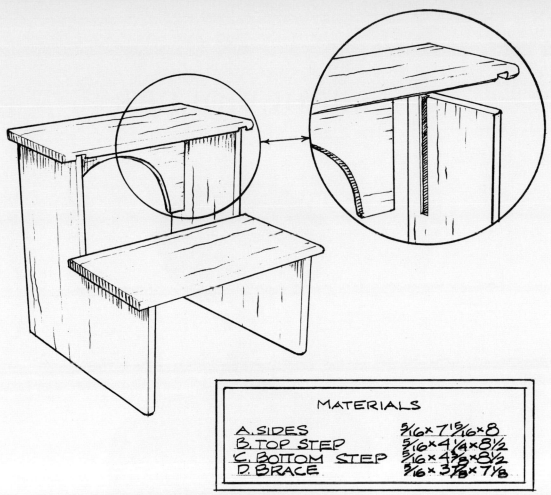

MATERIALS

A. SIDES	$5/16 \times 7^{15}/16 \times 8$
B. TOP STEP	$5/16 \times 4^{1}/4 \times 8^{1}/2$
C. BOTTOM STEP	$5/16 \times 4^{3}/8 \times 8^{1}/2$
D. BRACE	$5/16 \times 3^{7}/8 \times 7^{1}/8$

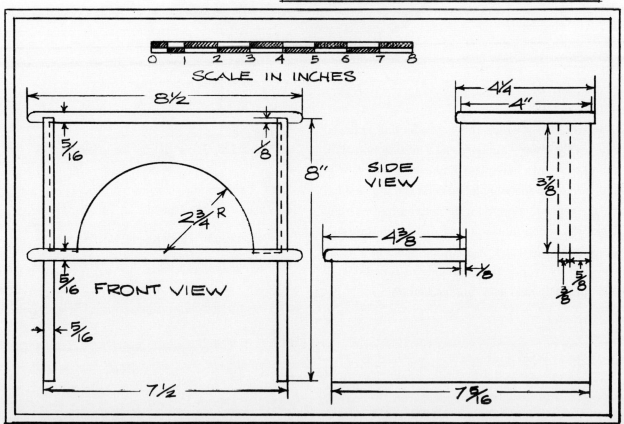

0 1 2 3 4 5 6 7 8

SCALE IN INCHES

$8^{1}/2$

$5/16$

$1/8$

$8''$

$2^{3}/4$ R

SIDE VIEW

$4^{1}/4''$

$4''$

$3^{7}/8$

$5/16$ FRONT VIEW

$4^{3}/8$

$1/8$

$5/16$

$3/8$

$5/16$

$7^{1}/2$

$7^{5}/16$

SPOOL HOLDER

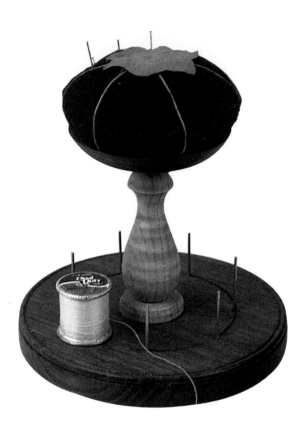

The original on which this reproduction is based (drawn by Ejner Handberg) is a bit different than the piece shown here. The pin cushion on the original is more noticeably lobed than the pin cushion on my reproduction, and the original pin cushion lacks the green fabric star. Also, on the original, there is a little wood fingertip fastened to a metal rod that protrudes from the side of the pedestal. This fingertip acts as a thimble holder.

Materials List

A.	Pedestal	1 pc.	1½ x 4¹³⁄₁₆
B.	Base	1 pc.	¹¹⁄₁₆ x 5⅞
C.	Dish	1 pc.	⁹⁄₁₆ x 3¾
D.	Brass rods	7 pcs.	¹⁄₁₆ x 1½
E.	Pin cushion	1 pc.	

Construction

I began by thicknessing the stock from which I would turn the dish and the base. After scribing slightly oversized circles on the stock with a compass, I band-sawed the disks from which these parts would be turned.

I started with the base. After screwing it to a three-inch faceplate, which I then mounted onto the drive center of my lathe, I turned the small bead atop the base's outside diameter. Then, with the point of my skew chisel, I cut the scoring on the top of the base. I then mounted the dish onto the faceplate so that its bottom side would be exposed to the lathe tools. After defining the curved underside of the dish, I removed the dish from the faceplate, turned it over, and remounted it so that I could turn the dished-out area in which the pin cushion would sit. (It's important that the screws be turned into the dish stock close enough to the center of the disk so that the holes made by the mounting screws won't be visible on the bottom side of the dish's rim.)

The last piece I turned was the pedestal. Although the pedestal's visible shapes were turned easily, the tenons at the top and bottom required extra consideration. I began the formation of each tenon with a parting tool, moving into the work until I'd reached the proper diameter. Then, with a gouge, I roughed in the remainder of each tenon, taking care not go in as deeply as the tenons' final diameters. Next, with a sharp paring chisel laid facedown on the tool rest, I scraped the full length of the tenons down to the finished diameter.

(Although it might be possible for you to make this spool holder without a drill press, I think a drill press makes success much more likely. Using the drillpress assures that the mortises will be aligned at right angles to the faces of both the dish and the base.)

Using my drill press, I bored the mortises in the base and the dish into which the pedestal's tenons would later fit. Then, before gluing the tenons into their mortises, I drilled the ¹⁄₁₆ inch holes into which the short brass rods (the spool holders) would fit. These, too, should be done on the drill press to ensure that the brass rods will stand up at right angles to the surface of the base.

I glued the pin cushion in place with white Elmer's glue after applying a finish to the assembled spool holder.

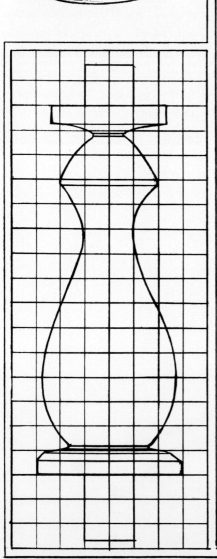

¼ GRID

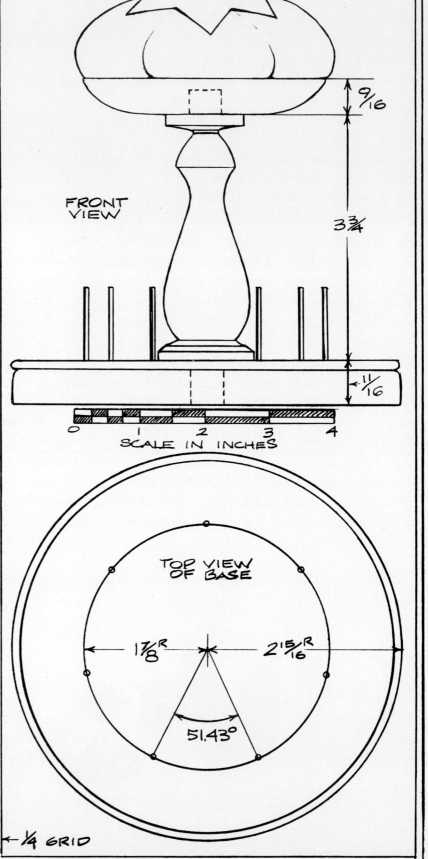

FRONT VIEW

$\frac{9}{16}$

$3\frac{3}{4}$

$\frac{11}{16}$

0   1   2   3   4

SCALE IN INCHES

TOP VIEW OF BASE

$1\frac{7}{8}$R

$2\frac{15}{16}$R

51.43°

HANGERS

These three simple forms require little in the way of materials and labor, but they are, nonetheless, attractive objects that can be used in the contemporary home. True, they can't be hung on a closet rod, but they will hang from the hooks or pegs often used in bathrooms and bedrooms.

Materials List

Hanger #1	1 pc.	½ x 1¹¹⁄₁₆ x 16¼
Hanger #2	1 pc.	½ x 2³⁄₁₆ x 16¼
Hanger #3	1 pc.	½ x 3⅜ x 16¼

Each requires a loop of leather.

Construction

After thicknessing the material, I band-sawed the profiles and shaped the edges with spokeshaves, rasps, and sandpaper.

I use a wooden-bodied spokeshave to create a gentle radius on the band-sawn edges of each hanger.

SCALE IN INCHES

0 1 2 3 4

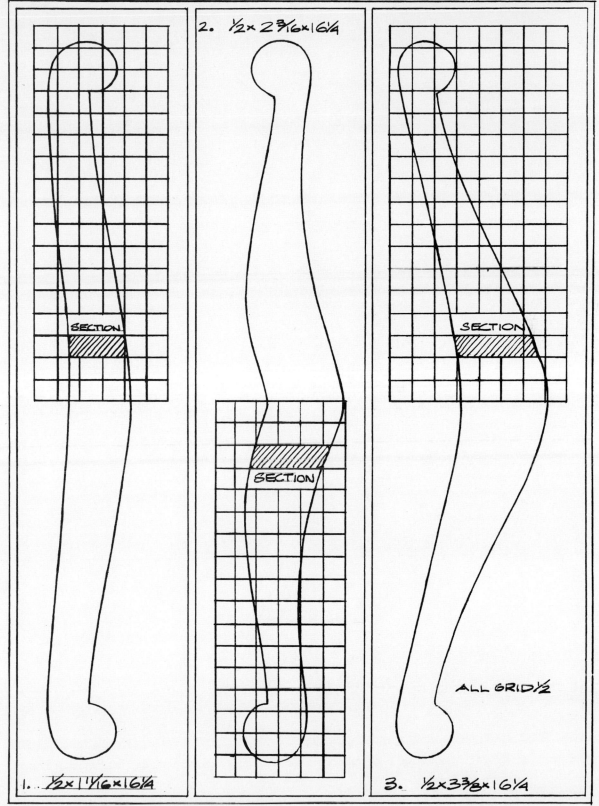

2. ½ × 2³⁄₁₆ × 16¼

SECTION

SECTION

SECTION

ALL GRID ½

1... ½ × 1¹⁄₁₆ × 16¼

3. ½ × 3³⁄₈ × 16¼

WOODENWARE FOR
∎ THE WORKROOM ∎

*T*he objects appearing in this section might have been used in any room. The candle box and the candle sconce would certainly have been at home in any location in which Shakers might have worked or read or talked after dark. The carriers, too, might have seen use in the kitchen or the sewing room. Certainly these are all objects which would have been at home in those rooms in which the Shakers worked at their many trades.

FIGURED OAK CANDLE BOX

The original box on which this piece is based has a lid fastened to the body of the box through the use of two pairs of staples with intertwined legs. The first version I built employed these staple hinges, but because there was so much play in movement of the staples, the lid didn't close with what I saw as an acceptable alignment. I switched then to a pair of tiny brass hinges.

Materials List

A. Sides   2 pcs. $\frac{3}{8}$ x $4\frac{3}{8}$ x $11\frac{7}{8}$

B. Ends   2 pcs. $\frac{3}{8}$ x $4\frac{3}{8}$ x $4\frac{3}{8}$

C. Bottom   1 pc. $\frac{3}{8}$ x $3\frac{5}{8}$ x $11\frac{1}{8}$

D. Lid   1 pc. $\frac{3}{8}$ x $4\frac{1}{2}$ x $12\frac{5}{16}$

E. Hinges   2 pcs.

F. Nails

Construction

After milling the material to the proper dimensions, I cut the dovetails and glued the body of the box together. I then slid the bottom into place, holding it there with friction and a dozen small nails. Before attaching the lid, I formed the bevel on the front and both ends of the lid, using a jack plane in much the same manner as that for the creation of the quarter round that decorates the bottom of the cherry two-compartment tray described earlier.

The lower leaves of the hinges were then mortised into the top edge of the box back. The upper leaves were simply screwed to the bottom side of the lid.

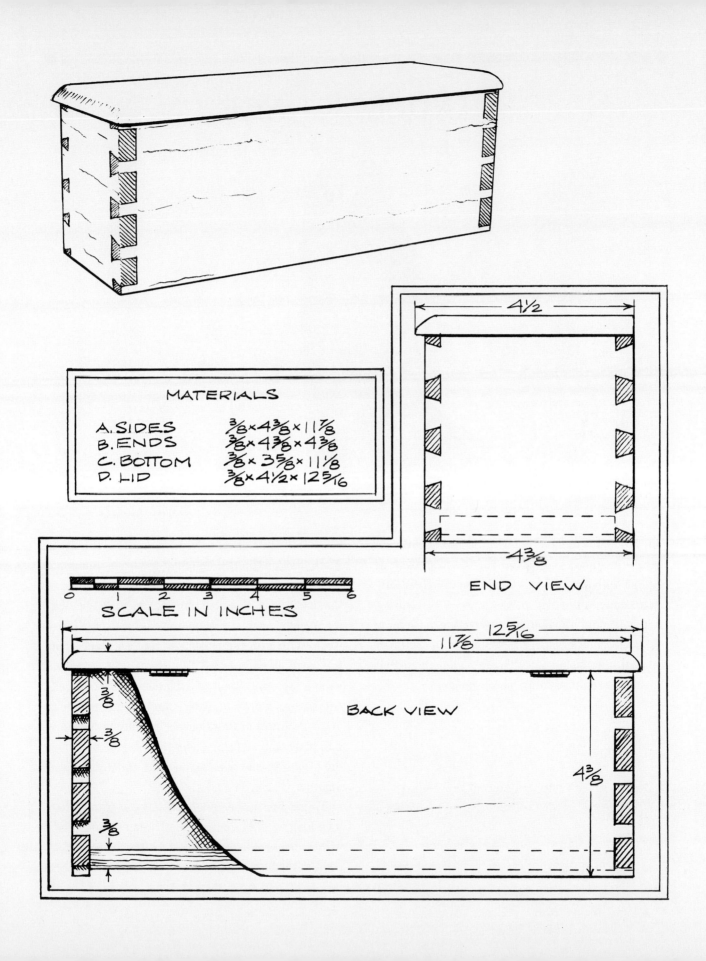

MATERIALS

A. SIDES $\frac{3}{8} \times 4\frac{3}{8} \times 11\frac{7}{8}$
B. ENDS $\frac{3}{8} \times 4\frac{3}{8} \times 4\frac{3}{8}$
C. BOTTOM $\frac{3}{8} \times 3\frac{5}{8} \times 11\frac{1}{8}$
D. LID $\frac{3}{8} \times 4\frac{1}{2} \times 12\frac{5}{16}$

$4\frac{1}{2}$

$4\frac{3}{8}$

END VIEW

0 1 2 3 4 5 6

SCALE IN INCHES

$12\frac{5}{16}$

$11\frac{7}{8}$

BACK VIEW

$\frac{3}{8}$

$\frac{3}{8}$

$\frac{3}{8}$

$4\frac{3}{8}$

CANDLE SCONCE

The original sconce on which this reproduction is based—it appears in John Kassay's *The Book of Shaker Furniture*—was made in the New Lebanon community early in the nineteenth century. On the original, the hole on which the sconce hung had been crudely enlarged, perhaps with a knife or a chisel, increasing the diameter enough so that the sconce could be hung on a large peg.

Materials List

A. Back	1 pc.	$\frac{5}{16}$ x $5\frac{9}{16}$ x $15\frac{11}{16}$
B. Sides	2 pcs.	$\frac{5}{16}$ x $6\frac{5}{16}$ x 12
C. Bottom	1 pc.	$\frac{5}{16}$ x $6\frac{3}{16}$ x $7\frac{1}{2}$
E. Front	1 pc.	$\frac{5}{16}$ x $1\frac{3}{16}$ x $8\frac{1}{8}$
F. Brads		

Construction

After thicknessing the lumber, I cut out the parts on my band saw. I then bored the one-inch hole in the back panel. Because the sides meet the back at a non-right angle, their union requires some fussy work. With a paring chisel and a block plane, I cut the bevel on each edge of the sconce back, establishing the upper limit of each bevel with one delicate pass of a dovetail saw. I made frequent checks of the accuracy of these bevels by holding the sides into place and sighting along the joint. Then, when the proper fit had been achieved, I nailed the piece together.

To get the proper angles, I left the front a half inch long on both ends. I then trimmed those ends with a dovetail saw and a plane, after the piece had been assembled.

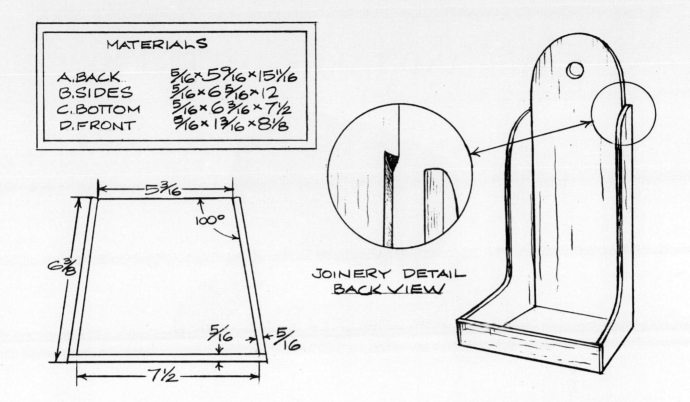

MATERIALS

A. BACK ... $5/16 \times 5\,9/16 \times 15\,11/16$
B. SIDES ... $5/16 \times 6\,5/16 \times 12$
C. BOTTOM ... $5/16 \times 6\,3/16 \times 7\,1/2$
D. FRONT ... $5/16 \times 1\,3/16 \times 8\,1/8$

$5\,3/16$

$100°$

$6\,3/8$

$5/16$ $5/16$

$7\,1/2$

JOINERY DETAIL
BACK VIEW

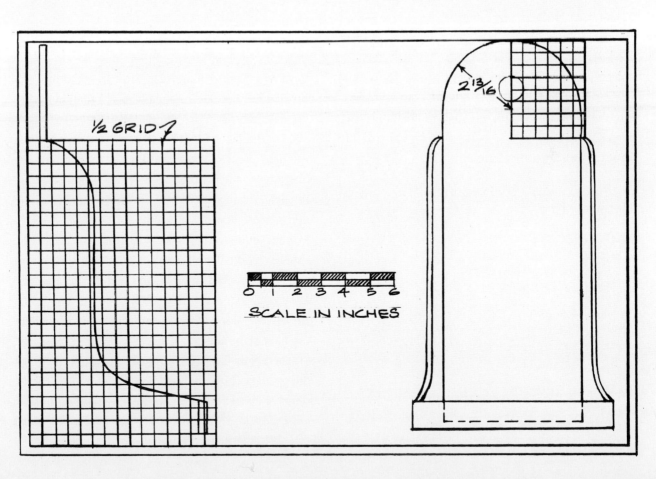

½ GRID

$2\,13/16$

0 1 2 3 4 5 6

SCALE IN INCHES

SMALL AND LARGE MALLETS

These two mallets are derived from examples shown in June Sprigg and Jim Johnson's *Shaker Woodenware: A Field Guide*, Volume 2. The authors make no guesses about the uses the smaller mallet might have seen. They do, however, theorize that—because of its unusual proportions—the larger mallet might have been used for several different woodshop applications.

Materials List

Small Mallet

A.	Head	1 pc.	1⅞ x 2½
B.	Handle	1 pc.	1¹⁄₁₆ x 5⅜
C.	Foxed wedge		pared to fit

Construction

I began by rough turning the heads on each mallet down to cylinders slightly greater in diameter than the diameter of the finished heads. I then moved to the drill press.

I set the fence on my drill press a distance from the lead point of my Forstner bit that is half the diameter of the head being mortised. Then, holding the head against the fence, I drilled a mortise of the appropriate depth.

I remounted the heads in the lathe, cut the tapers, planed and sanded the surfaces, and placed the scored lines. I then turned the handles. (*See* page 81 on the construction of the Spool Holder for more about forming the tenons at the top of each handle.)

The heads could have been fastened to the handles with nothing more than a glued and tightly fit tenon. I chose, however, to use a variation of that joint which, I felt, would give me a bit more strength: the foxed wedge.

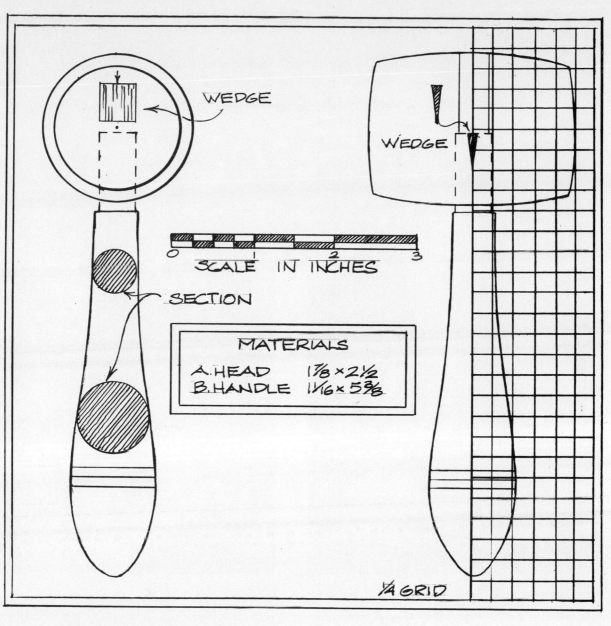

WEDGE

WEDGE

SCALE IN INCHES

0   1   2   3

SECTION

MATERIALS

A. HEAD $1\frac{7}{8} \times 2\frac{1}{2}$
B. HANDLE $1\frac{1}{16} \times 5\frac{3}{8}$

¼ GRID

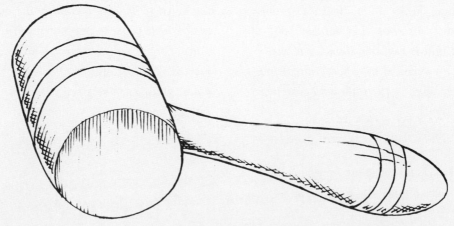

The foxed wedge is defined as a blind mortise housing a tenon into which is cut a notch occupied by a slightly oversized wedge. When the tenon is tapped into the mortise, the top of the oversized wedge strikes the bottom of the mortise. This action drives the wedge more deeply into the tenon which presses the sides more tightly against the walls of the mortise.

Materials List
Large Mallet

A. Head	1 pc.	3¼ x 5¹⁄₁₆
B. Handle	1 pc.	1¹⁄₁₆ x 5⁹⁄₁₆
C. Foxed wedge		pared to fit

The head of the large mallet has been rough turned to a cylinder. I then remove the cylinder from the lathe. Placing the cylinder on my drill press table with the fence set a distance from the lead point of the Forstner bit that is half the diameter of the cylinder, I bore a mortise of the appropriate depth. I then remount the head in the lathe and complete the turning.

A walnut wedge has been fitted into the notch cut into the end of the handle tenon. When the top of the notch strikes the bottom of the mortise (in the mallet head), the wedge is driven further into the notch, spreading the tenon against the walls of the mortise. This action locks the tenon permanently in place. (All parts are glued before the tenon is fit into the mortise.)

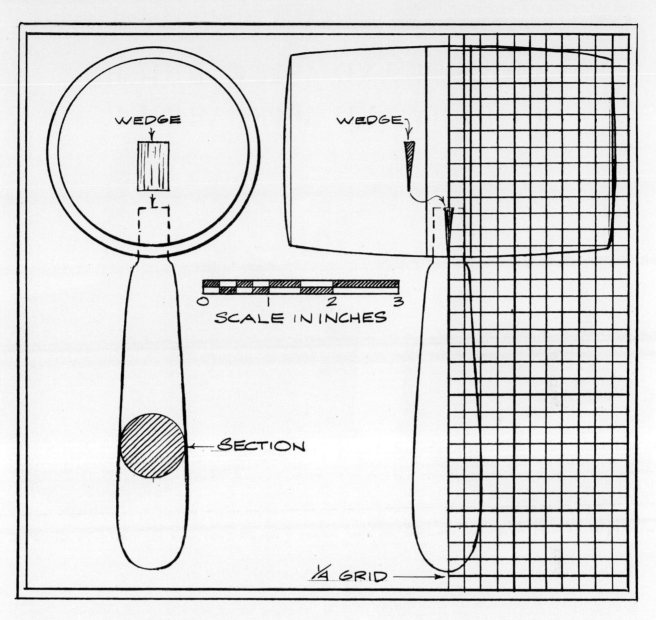

WEDGE

WEDGE

SECTION

SCALE IN INCHES

0   1   2   3

¼ GRID

MATERIALS

A. HEAD   3¼ × 5⅛
B. HANDLE   1⅛ × 5⁹⁄₁₆

WALNUT AND ASH CARRIER
CHERRY AND ASH CARRIER

These delicate little carriers are simple to build and provide a painless introduction to the wood-bending process.

Materials List

Smaller Carrier

A. Sides	2 pcs.	³⁄₁₆ x 2 x 5⅜	
B. Ends	2 pcs.	³⁄₁₆ x 23⁵⁄₁₆	
C. Bottom	1 pc.	³⁄₁₆ x 3³⁄₁₆ x 5⅝	
D. Handle	1 pc.	⅛ x ⅜ x 10	
E. Copper tacks	4 pcs.		
F. Brads			

Construction

Because the bent-wood handles require several days of curing time, I started by preparing the ash stock for bending. First, I selected some clear, straight-grained material, which I then resawed and planed down to a bit less than ⅛ inch. Because the tight radii the handles require could result in bending failure, I prepared more strips than I would actually need. I next band-sawed the bending forms on which the handles would cure. I made two sizes, one for the smaller walnut-bodied carrier and a larger size for the cherry-bodied carrier. When my preparations had been completed, I turned my attention to the actual bending process.

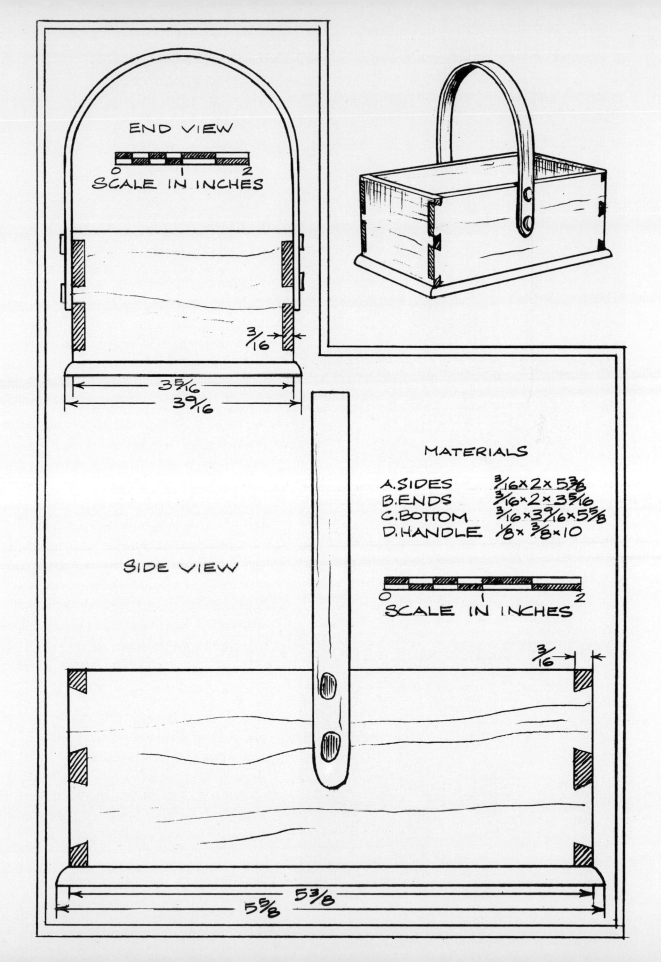

END VIEW

SCALE IN INCHES
0   1   2

3/16

3 5/16
3 9/16

SIDE VIEW

MATERIALS

A. SIDES   3/16 × 2 × 5 3/8
B. ENDS   3/16 × 2 × 3 5/16
C. BOTTOM   3/16 × 3 9/16 × 5 5/8
D. HANDLE   1/8 × 3/8 × 10

SCALE IN INCHES
0   1   2

3/16

5 5/8
5 3/8

This photo shows the steamer in which I plasticize my handle stock. The water is heated in the french frier. Steam is then directed up into the length of PVC, which contains the parts being prepared for bending.

Materials List
Larger Carrier

A.	Sides	2 pcs.	3⁄16 x 3 x 8
B.	Ends	2 pcs.	3⁄16 x 3 x 51⁄16
C.	Bottom	1 pc.	3⁄16 x 55⁄16 x 81⁄4
D.	Handle	1 pc.	1⁄8 x 1⁄2 x 143⁄4
E.	Copper tacks		4 pcs.
F.	Brads		

Bending can occur when the wood has been plasticized enough to assume the desired shape without breaking. There are two different ways to plasticize wood—both using water as the softening agent. Boiling the strips is perhaps the easiest method in this particular case, because these strips are small enough to fit into a stove-top pan. (I chose to steam mine because I have already made a steamerthat I use to plasticize post and slat stock in my chairmaking shop.)

After steaming the strips for 30 to 40 minutes, I removed them from the steamer and—working quickly but carefully—moved to the bending forms, where I wrapped the steamed strips of ash into place. Then I secured them to the forms with clamps.

After removing them from the steamer, I wrap the ash strips around the bending forms. Notice that each form is wrapped with two strips. (One of the two strips wrapped around the larger form failed, breaking out on its outside surface. Such failure is relatively rare for a good bending wood like ash.)

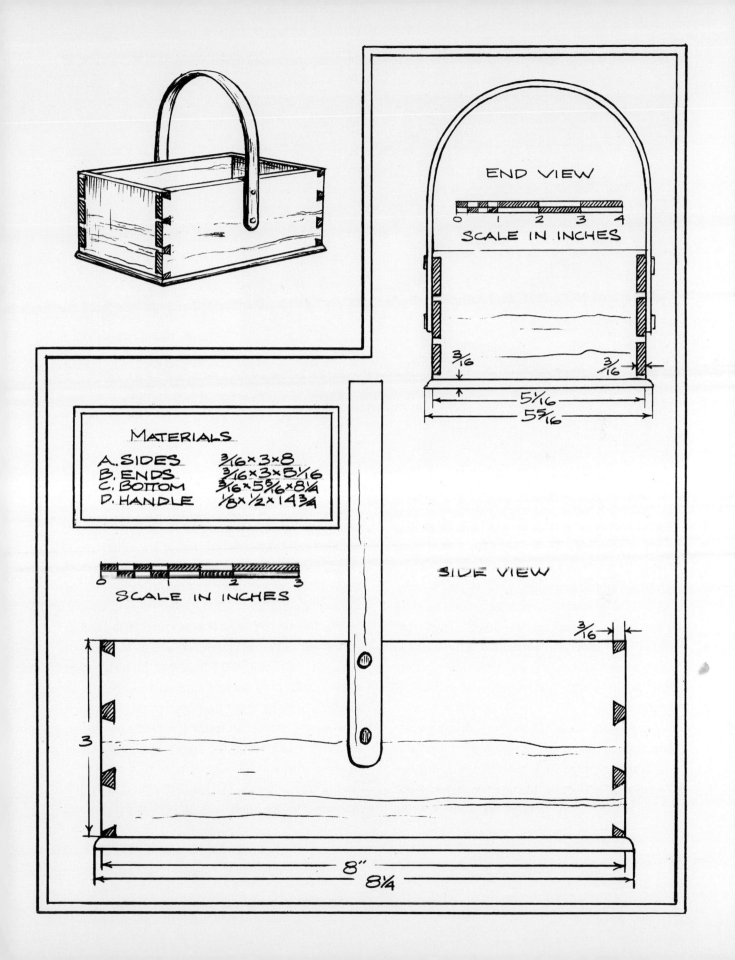

END VIEW

SCALE IN INCHES
0   1   2   3   4

3/16

3/16

5¹⁄₁₆

5⁵⁄₁₆

MATERIALS

A. SIDES   3/16 × 3 × 8
B. ENDS   3/16 × 3 × 5¹⁄₁₆
C. BOTTOM   3/16 × 5⁵⁄₁₆ × 8¼
D. HANDLE   ⅛ × ½ × 14¾

SCALE IN INCHES
0   1   2   3

SIDE VIEW

3/16

3

8"

8¼

Holding the parts in the proper alignment by means of spring clamps, I pre-drill holes for the tacks that will hold the handles in place.

I next turned my attention to the construction of the boxes. Because I was working from photos (*Shaker Woodenware: A Field Guide,* Volume 1) and not measured drawings, I had to make guesses about the material thicknesses. Working from the only given measurements—height, length, and width of the carriers—I estimated a thickness of $\frac{3}{16}$ inch for the wall material of the smaller carrier and a thickness of $\frac{5}{32}$ inch for the wall material of the larger carrier.

After planing the stock to these thicknesses, I began making the boxes. Although after assembly these are very durable constructions, individual parts are quite fragile during the construction process. The pins and tails that constitute dovetail joinery are particularly delicate and so must be handled carefully.

After dovetailing the sides together, I fastened the bottoms into place with brads (after predrilling the brad holes.).

The handle on the Shaker original of the smaller box was held in place with copper tacks that had been clinched over on the inside of the box. I used larger tacks than those found on the original in order to be sure that I had enough tack to clinch over on the inside. Although the swing handle on the Shaker original of the larger carrier was held in place with a single copper rivet on each side, I used a pair of tacks, fastening that handle in the same way as the handles on the smaller boxes.

I drive the copper tacks through the pre-drilled holes and bend them over against the flat saw wrench that is clamped to my bench extension. (In order to get the tacks to bend over in the same direction, I start them on their way with a pair of pliers, after driving them through the side-wall material but before peening them against the wrench.)

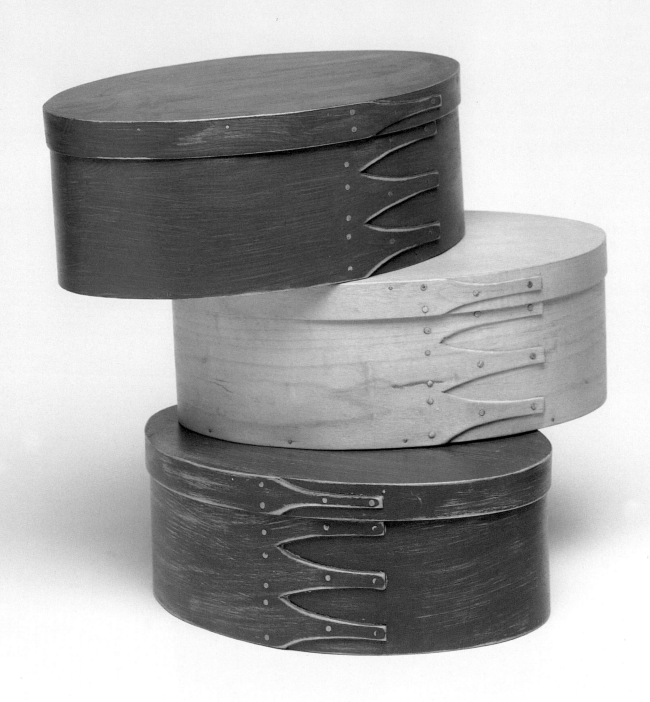

WOODENWARE FOR
▪ THE STORAGE ROOM ▪

The oval box, the quintessential item of Shaker woodenware, could have been used in any room in which Shakers lived and worked; however, since its obvious function was storage, I have chosen to identify it as an item seeing the greatest use in the storage room.

OVAL BOXES

The Shakers made bentwood boxes in a bewildering array of sizes and shapes. Some have lids, like those appearing on these pages. Others have handles but no lids and were used as carriers. Still others have neither handles nor lids. Spit boxes are among the forms fitting into this last category.

Materials

Maple was the preferred material for the sides of Shaker bentwood boxes, as it is readily bent, in addition to being very strong even when planed to a thickness of ⅟16 inch or less. Vertical-grained pine was the material of choice for the tops and bottoms of these boxes. Vertical-grained pine (quarter-sawn material) is stable and unlikely to warp, an important consideration when creating parts that can't be pinned into place against sturdy structural members. I used maple and vertical-grained pine in each of the boxes appearing here.

I resawed and planed to thickness some of the material I used for box sides; however, recognizing that not every reader has access to a band saw with resaw capacity, I also built several boxes using ⅟16-inch maple veneer (available from many suppliers). Both types of material worked just fine.

No. 2 construction-grade white pine was used for the tops and bottoms. By sorting through the material at my local lumber supplier, I was able to pick out some boards exhibiting a vertical grain (on the top and bottom of the board the grain lines appear straight, parallel, and closely spaced) across most of their width. I then cut around the defects—knots, pitch pockets, unpredictable grain—and planed down to a thickness of ½ inch. Then I stickered it and allowed it to sit for several months in my warm, dry shop. Finally, with a jack plane, I flattened any curl on one side, then fed the material into my planer with the flat side down, reducing the thickness to the ¼ inch needed.

Construction

Although I had a fair amount of experience making bentwood boxes, I had never before made any of the distinctive Shaker oval boxes. As a result, I had to start from ground zero.

Molds

My first concern was the construction of the molds. These are the forms on which the softened box and lid sides will be wrapped and allowed to dry. In *Shaker Woodenware: A Field Guide*, June Sprigg and Jim Johnson present one of the molds used by the Shakers in the construction of oval boxes. The seven-inch oval form sits atop a shaft that could be locked into a vise to hold the mold securely. Let into the front face of the mold are a pair of cast-iron strips against which the copper tacks which hold the box sides together were peened. The molds I designed, although different in several details, are very similar in use.

Each box required two molds, one for the box itself and one for the lid. Both molds have a metal strip let into its front side directly under the position of the lap on the finished box.

I selected walnut and cherry for my mold woods because these were the species I had in sufficient thicknesses (any species would work). After band-sawing the box mold material to the proper shape, I worked the material with a block plane, rasps, and sandpaper to smooth and regularize the surfaces. (Remember that as the height of the boxes varies so too does the thickness of the box molds.) It's important that these molds be accurately shaped, because any error can result in unsightly flat spots in the walls of the finished boxes. When the proper shape had been achieved, I then screwed a 2 x 4 block to the bottom of each mold to allow it to be held in place in my vise during the wrapping and tacking processes.

The box mold in the background has been given a sheet-metal insert against which the copper tacks will be peened. The lid mold, which is clamped in my bench vise in the foreground, is ready to have its sheet-metal insert cemented into the recess cut into its outside diameter.

After finishing the box molds, I made the molds for the lids. (Remember that these too will vary in thickness.) To get the right size, I traced the outside of each box mold and added 1/16 inch all the way around. I then band-sawed the profile and finished each shape with hand tools. I screwed 2 x 4 blocks to the bottoms of these molds also.

The next step was the installation of the metal strips on the front wall of each mold against which the copper tacks would be peened. I didn't have the thin cast iron used by the Shakers, but one of the contractors then working on our roof pulled off a length of galvanized drip edge dating back to the 1960s. It was a much heavier gauge metal than would be seen today. I plucked this drip edge from the scrap heap and began cutting metal strips.

Then, with a paring chisel, I cut the shallow recessed surfaces into which the metal would be placed. After thoroughly coating both the back of the metal and the recessed areas in the molds with contact cement, I pressed each piece into its place.

Boxes

I used a fine-toothed ¹⁄₁₆-inch band-saw blade to rip to width the strips needed for box and lid sides. I then planed the sawn edges of these strips. To do this, I clamped the strips between two lengths of ½-inch material so that the sawn edge of the strips extended a bit beyond the edges of the boards. This provided the thin strips with enough support to permit planing.

Next, I cut the strips to the needed length, again using the ¹⁄₁₆-inch band-saw blade.

I cut the distinctive fingers of the oval boxes by hand, using a sharp knife. Although requiring some effort, this is not as difficult as it may sound. First, I spring-clamped the strip to a board laid across my bench. Then, after one light scoring cut to establish the line, two or three power cuts separated the fingers from the waste.

I used a sharp chisel drug backwards across the surface of the material to clean up any irregularities, as well as to diminish the thickness of the lapped parts. (The two smaller boxes should be made of stock a bit thinner than the ¹⁄₁₆-inch sidewall material of the larger boxes.) The box and lid sides were then ready for soaking.

Materials List
Smallest Box

A.	Box side	1 pc.	³⁄₆₄ x 1⅜ x 11¾
B.	Lid side	1 pc.	³⁄₆₄ x 7/16 x 11¾
C.	Box bottom	1 pc.	³⁄₁₆ x 2¼ x 3½
D.	Lid top	1 pc.	³⁄₁₆ x 2⅜ 3⅝
E.	Copper tacks		
F.	Brads		

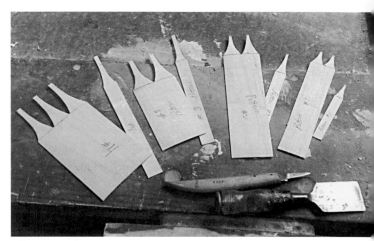

These are the patterns I trace onto my box and lid sides prior to cutting their fingers.

A block plane is used to clean up the sawn edges of the strips that will become box and lid sides.

I use a very sharp chisel as a scraper to reduce the thickness of the lapped ends of the sides.

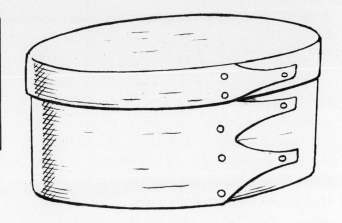

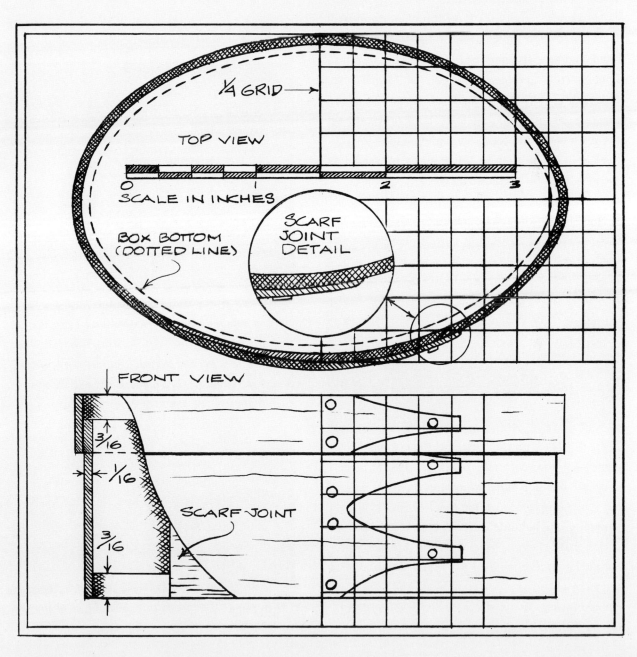

1/4 GRID →

TOP VIEW

SCALE IN INCHES

0   1   2   3

BOX BOTTOM
(DOTTED LINE)

SCARF
JOINT
DETAIL

FRONT VIEW

3/16

1/16

3/16

SCARF JOINT

I tried doing this in both hot and cold water. I tried one-hour soaks, and I tried overnight soaks, and no approach seemed better than any other approach. Each of these techniques permitted the thin maple to bend very readily. I didn't use steam because I was afraid that that might cause the thin pieces of material to curl up too tightly to be saved. Plus, I have heard that the Shakers, themselves, soaked rather than steamed their box sides.

My first attempts to wrap the plasticized wall material around the molds didn't go very well. As I struggled with the material, it invariably began to split in the notches between the fingers. My Solution? I decided to hold the fingers in place under cauls made of four thin strips of wood held together with duct tape. The band clamps (or rubber bands) were then wrapped around these cauls (seen in the bottom photo on page 113.)

The 2 x 4 block on the bottom of the box mold is clamped in my bench vise, which permits me to wrap the box side material around the mold without struggling to control the mold's position. After wrapping, the box side material is held in place with a band clamp. (To hold all the side material on all the smaller molds, I use rubber bands. Notice the piece of waxed paper underneath the metal clamp bracket. This keeps the metal from staining the wet maple.)

Materials List
Small Box

A.	Box side	1 pc.	$3/64$ x 2 x $17 1/16$
B.	Lid side	1 pc.	$3/64$ x $9/16$ x $17 1/8$
C.	Box bottom	1 pc.	$3/16$ x $3 1/8$ x $4 15/16$
D.	Lid top	1 pc.	$3/16$ x $3 1/4$ x $5 1/16$
E.	Copper tacks		
F.	Brads		

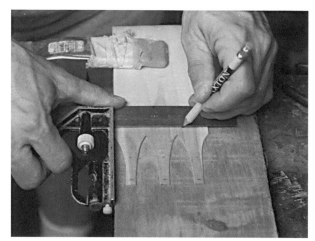

After twenty-four hours wrapped around the mold, the box side material is removed and I prepare to tack the ends together. After spring-clamping the material to a backup board, I square three lines across the fingers. The copper tacks will be positioned along these lines.

I then pre-drill through this outer layer of lap for each tack.

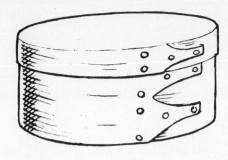

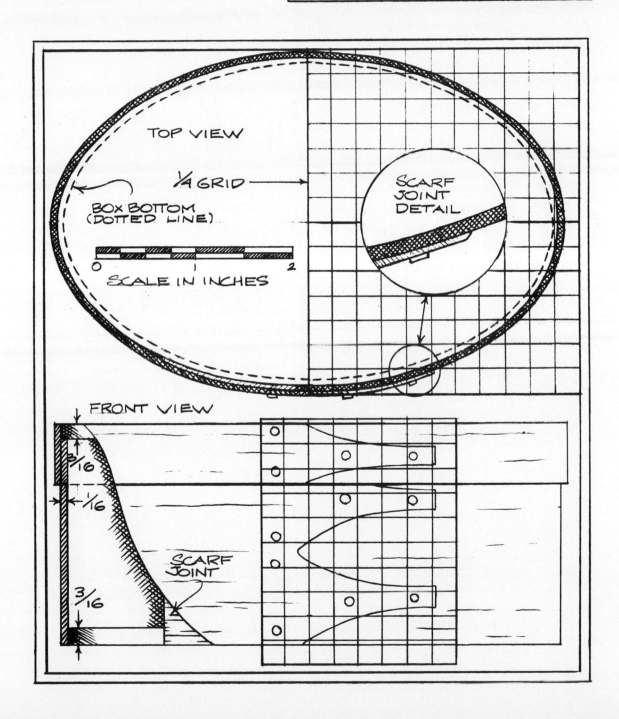

MATERIALS

A. BOX SIDE	$\frac{1}{16} \times 2 \times 17\frac{1}{16}$
B. LID SIDE	$\frac{1}{16} \times \frac{9}{16} \times 17\frac{1}{8}$
C. BOX BOTTOM	$\frac{3}{16} \times 3\frac{1}{8} \times 4\frac{15}{16}$
D. LID TOP	$\frac{3}{16} \times 3\frac{3}{4} \times 5\frac{1}{16}$

TOP VIEW

$\frac{1}{4}$ GRID

BOX BOTTOM
(DOTTED LINE)

0   1   2
SCALE IN INCHES

SCARF
JOINT
DETAIL

FRONT VIEW

$\frac{3}{16}$

$\frac{1}{16}$

$\frac{3}{16}$

SCARF
JOINT

After struggling to tack a freshly soaked piece of box side material, I decided to switch to a two-part system of bending.

I started by wrapping the material tightly around the mold, then holding it in place for twenty-four hours through the use of web clamps or large rubber bands. Then, after the bend had begun to set, I removed the box side material and pre-drilled the tack holes in the outer layer of lap.

Next, I rewrapped the material around the mold, which this time was held in the jaws of a Quick-Grip clamp the bar of which was locked into my bench vise in order to hold the mold at a convenient working height. I then tacked the lap together and allowed it to set another twenty-four hours before installing tops and bottoms.

It's important that the lap be tacked directly over the metal insert in the box mold. It's only there that the ends of the tacks can be peened over, locking the lap tightly in place.

The Shaker craftsmen who made oval boxes used only these tiny tacks to hold the lapped ends

Materials List
Large Box

A.	Box side	1 pc.	$\frac{1}{16}$ x $2\frac{3}{8}$ x $20\frac{11}{16}$
B.	Lid side	1 pc.	$\frac{1}{16}$ x $\frac{5}{8}$ x 21
C.	Box bottom	1 pc.	$\frac{1}{4}$ x $4\frac{3}{16}$ x $6\frac{1}{8}$
D.	Lid top	1 pc.	$\frac{1}{4}$ x $4\frac{5}{16}$ x $6\frac{1}{4}$
E.	Copper tacks		
F.	Brads		

of the box sides together. I, however, couldn't resist slathering on a bit of glue, although I don't think it's really necessary. Early on in my construction of these boxes, while attempting to fit a freshly glued and tacked lid hoop over a pine lid disk that was just a bit too large (remember: the glue had not yet set) I realized that I was pulling at that hoop with all the strength in my fingers, and the tacks did not surrender their grip.

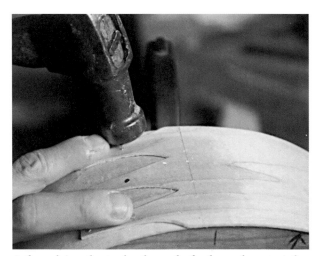

The box mold is shown clamped in the jaws of the Quick-Grip clamp. The bottom of the bar is then held in my bench vise. This arrangement presents the metal-sided face of the mold in the proper position for tacking.

I then drive the tacks through the lapped material, finishing each drive with a firm blow to peen over the end of the tack against the metal insert on the box mold. (The two pencil lines below the lapped fingers show the position of the metal insert.)

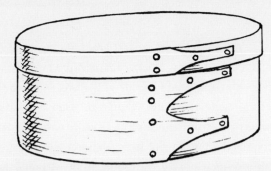

MATERIALS	
A. BOX SIDE	$\frac{1}{16} \times 2\frac{3}{8} \times 20\frac{11}{16}$
B. LID SIDE	$\frac{1}{16} \times \frac{5}{8} \times 21$
C. BOX BOTTOM	$\frac{1}{4} \times 4\frac{3}{16} \times 6\frac{1}{8}$
D. LID TOP	$\frac{1}{4} \times 4\frac{5}{16} \times 6\frac{1}{4}$

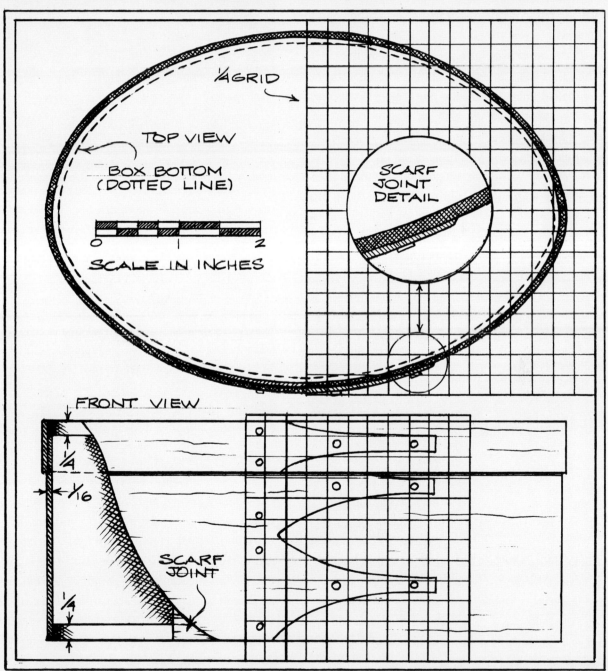

$\frac{1}{4}$ GRID

TOP VIEW

BOX BOTTOM
(DOTTED LINE)

0   1   2
SCALE IN INCHES

SCARF
JOINT
DETAIL

FRONT VIEW

$\frac{1}{4}$

$\frac{1}{16}$

SCARF
JOINT

$\frac{1}{4}$

I set the dry and tacked box side material on a piece of ¼-inch thick, vertical-grain pine and traced around the interior of the box with a pencil. Then, very carefully, using a ¼-inch band-saw blade, I cut out the bottom. The first few bottoms required some fitting with a plane and a rasp, but eventually I got to the point where I could move directly from the band saw to the installation of the bottom.

The bottom was then pressed into the box side walls and held there with brads driven through pre-drilled holes in the side material. The Shakers used wooden pegs, as well as copper tacks and brads for this task.

I next turned my attention to the lid.

First, I wrapped the unfastened lid side material around the outside top of the box. When the material had been wrapped snugly, I marked the end of the lap with a pencil. Then, moving to the lid mold (which was held in the jaws of a Quick-Grip clamp like the box mold mentioned above), I tacked the ends of the lid side material together.

After tracing around the exterior of the box sides (to get the profile of the lid disk), the location of the ends of the fingers is marked.

The lid side material is wrapped around the top of the assembled box. A pencil line is then placed on the material to indicate the correct position of the lap. The material is then taken to the lid mold (held in the jaws of a Quick-Grip clamp) and tacked together.

The lid hoop is then placed on the pine and positioned so that the end of its finger matches the mark on the pine. Holding it in that position, the end of the inside lap is then marked. This mark—the one to which the pencil points—indicates the placement of the relieved area that is later cut in the edge of the lid disk. This relieved area registers hoop placement, which positions the lid finger directly above the box fingers.

The first few times I made lids, I simply laid this hoop of lid side material onto a piece of ¼-inch-thick pine and traced a line on the inside of the hoop. But although this method worked and produced tightly fitting lid disks, sometimes the finger on the lid didn't align with those on the box. To correct this, I began using the tail of the lid hoop as a registration point, aligning its shallow notch on the edge of the lid disk to force the hoop into a position that brought the finger on the lid into alignment with those on the box front.

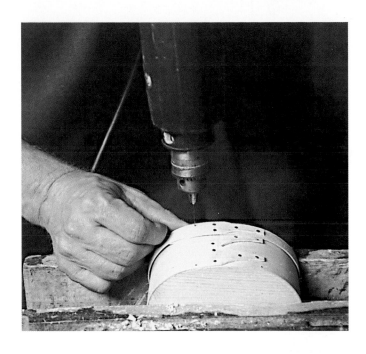

After pre-drilling the holes, the lid disk is bradded into place.

The boxes on the left are ready for finishing. The lid and box molds in the back are wrapped in material prior to tacking. The strips of wood on the right are box and lid sides. Notice the 2 x 4 blocks screwed to the base of each mold. Notice, too, the cauls on each set of box fingers. Without those cauls to hold the fingers flat during the wrapping process, splits can easily occur between the fingers. I make the cauls from strips of ¼-inch-thick material that is then held together with duct tape.

Later, as I made more boxes, I realized that if I was careful enough when I aligned the material on my lid mold, I could get it very nearly right in the first place and would then need to make only the slightest correction with the placement of the tail of the lid hoop to get the lid and box fingers properly aligned.

The lid hoop was then forced over the lid disk, and that disk was bradded into place through pre-drilled holes in the maple hoop.

Finishing

Four of the oval boxes I made for this book were given a natural finish using a concoction made of equal parts boiled linseed oil, mineral spirits, and polyurethane. This mixture was brushed on, allowed to get tacky, then wiped off. But because I had seen and liked many of the colored, antique Shaker oval boxes, I decided to experiment with some painted finishes.

Several boxes were painted with a quick-drying craft paint, which was then lightly sanded to reveal the high points of fingers and edges. Over this paint I then applied the same clear finish I had given the other boxes.

On two of the boxes, I applied two layers of contrasting paint, one over the other, which I then lightly sanded. This time the sanding revealed not only the natural wood but also the buried color.

Materials List
Largest Box

A. Box side   1 pc. $\frac{1}{16}$ x $3\frac{3}{16}$ x $28\frac{3}{8}$

B. Lid side   1 pc. $\frac{1}{16}$ x $\frac{3}{4}$ x $28\frac{1}{4}$

C. Box bottom   1 pc. $\frac{1}{4}$ x $5\frac{15}{16}$ x $8\frac{11}{16}$

D. Lid top   1 pc. $\frac{1}{4}$ x $6\frac{1}{8}$ x $8\frac{7}{8}$

E. Copper tacks

F. Brads

After painting, the boxes are lightly sanded with 220-grit paper to reveal high points. This gives the boxes an antique look.

MATERIALS
A. BOX SIDE   1/16 × 3 3/16 × 28 3/8
B. LID SIDE   1/16 × 3/4 × 28 1/4
C. BOX BOTTOM   1/4 × 5 13/16 × 8 11/16
D. LID TOP   1/4 × 6 1/8 × 8 7/8

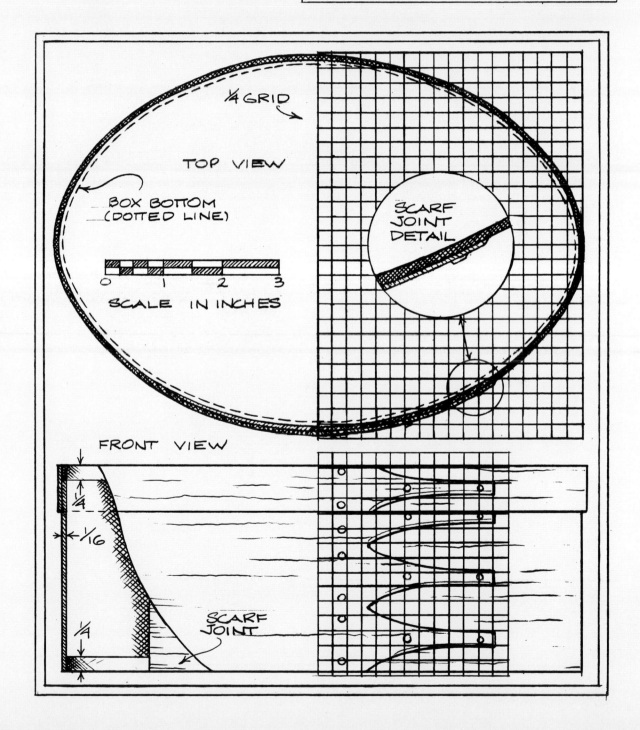

1/4 GRID

TOP VIEW

BOX BOTTOM
(DOTTED LINE)

0   1   2   3
SCALE IN INCHES

SCARF
JOINT
DETAIL

FRONT VIEW

1/4

1/16

1/4

SCARF
JOINT

▪ GALLERY ▪

GEORGE ROGERS

Harrodsburg, Kentucky

"Each piece I make, whether it's functional or art,
reflects the history of the tree from which it came.
My mission is to reveal that history through a piece that is a
pleasure for others to use and to feel."

Working primarily in cherry, George produces a line of household accessories in his Harrodsburg, Kentucky, shop.

Candle box

Oval box with handle

Carrier

Drying rack

Oval Boxes

CAMERON P. VAN DYKE

Grand Rapids, Michigan

*"In my work as a cabinetmaker I strive to produce work
of lasting beauty and integrity, making sure that each piece
performs its function to the highest efficiency.
These same ideals make for the beautiful simplicity
of the work of the Shakers."*

Set of Green Boxes
(Photo by Ted Boelema)

Set of Cherry Boxes
(Photo by Ted Boelema)

JOHN WILSON

Oval Boxmaker
Charlotte, Michigan

"Process is much more interesting to me than the product itself.
True, the product claims our attention because it is tangible,
but the process by which it is created is the life that produces it.
Focusing on process spares us from the tedium of material acquisition.
It is the line between craftsmen and collectors."

In addition to the many fine boxes he makes each year, John teaches
boxmaking in workshops across the country. He also sells boxmaking materials.

*The sidewalls of this tall box—the work of John
Wilson—are made of quarter-sawn American
sycamore, while the lid (and bottom)
are made of cherry.*

*Another example of John Wilson's work,
this shallow lidded box is made of bird's-eye
maple and walnut burl.*

▪ BIBLIOGRAPHY ▪

Allen, Douglas R., and Jerry V. Grant. *Shaker Furniture Makers*. Hanover, NH: University of New England Press, 1989.

Andrews, Edward Deming, and Faith Andrews. *Shaker Furniture: The Craftsmanship of an American Sect*. New York: Dover Publications, Inc., 1964.

Handberg, Ejner. *Measured Drawings of Shaker Furniture and Woodenware*. Stockbridge, MA: The Berkshire Traveler Press, 1980.

———. *Shop Drawings of Shaker Furniture and Woodenware*, Vols. 1, 2, 3 Stockbridge, MA: The Berkshire Traveler Press, 1973–91.

Johnson, Jim, and June Sprigg. *Shaker Woodenware: A Field Guide*, Vols. 1 and 2. Great Barrington, MA: Berkshire House, 1991 and 1992.

Kassay, John. *The Book of Shaker Furniture*. Amherst, MA: The University of Massachusetts Press, 1980.

Larkin, David, and June Sprigg. *Shaker Life, Work, and Art*. Boston: Houghton Mifflin, 1989.

Muller, Charles R., and Timothy D. Rieman. *The Shaker Chair*. Amherst, MA: The University of Massachusetts Press, 1992.

Rieman, Timothy D. *Shaker: The Art of Craftsmanship*. Alexandria, VA: Art Services International, 1995.

▪METRIC EQUIVALENTS▪

inches	mm	cm	inches	cm	inches	cm
⅛	3	0.3	9	22.9	30	76.2
¼	6	0.6	10	25.4	31	78.7
⅜	10	1.0	11	27.9	32	81.3
½	13	1.3	12	30.5	33	83.8
⅝	16	1.6	13	33.0	34	86.4
¾	19	1.9	14	35.6	35	88.9
⅞	22	2.2	15	38.1	36	91.4
1	25	2.5	16	40.6	37	94.0
1¼	32	3.2	17	43.2	38	96.6
1½	38	3.8	18	45.7	39	99.1
1¾	44	4.4	19	48.3	40	101.6
2	51	5.1	20	50.8	41	104.1
2½	64	6.4	21	53.3	42	106.7
3	76	7.6	22	55.9	43	109.2
3½	89	8.9	23	58.4	44	111.8
4	102	10.2	24	61.0	45	114.3
4½	114	11.4	25	63.5	46	116.8
5	127	12.7	26	66.0	47	119.4
6	152	15.2	27	68.6	48	121.9
7	178	17.8	28	71.1	49	124.5
8	203	20.3	29	73.7	50	127.0

mm = millimeter
cm = centimeter
m = meter

Foot and Inch Conversions
1 inch = 25.4 mm
1 foot = 304.8 mm

Metric Conversions
1 mm = 0.039 inch
1 m = 3.28 feet

■ ABOUT THE AUTHOR ■

Kerry Pierce is a teacher and a professional woodworker who has run his own custom woodshop and is currently contributing editor to *Woodwork* magazine. Kerry lives in Lancaster, Ohio, with his wife, Elaine, their daughter, Emily, and their son, Andy.

Kerry graduated in 1975 from Bowling Green State University, Bowling Green, Ohio, with a B.A. in English, and has been a teacher of secondary English in Texas and currently in Ohio. His interest in woodworking developed to the level that he opened is own custom woodshop in 1980, specializing in chair-making. In 1991, he received his Master of Arts degree in Art from Ohio University in Athens, Ohio.

Kerry is the author of five books on woodworking including this and his 1998 *The Art of Chair-Making,* also published by Sterling Publishing Co., Inc. He has been contributing editor to *Woodwork* magazine since 1995, and has published more than a dozen articles in *Woodwork* and more than a half-dozen in *Woodshop News* and *Weekend Woodcraft*. His story "Using a Portable Bandsaw Mill to Cut Graded Cabinet Lumber" in the June 1995, issue No. 33, of *Woodwork* was recently awarded the Stanley Tool Golden Hammer Award by the NAHWW (National Association of Home and Workshop Writers) for outstanding work in the field of home and workshop writing. The prize included a cash award as well as a selection of Stanley tools and other incidentals. Kerry especially enjoys writing profiles of other woodworkers, examining their techniques and showcasing their work. Recent profiles include "Brian Boggs: A Commitment to Excellence" in the February 1998, No. 49, *Woodwork*, and "Rob Gartzka and Kathie Johnson: Art or Furniture?" in the October 1997, No. 47, *Woodwork*.

∎ INDEX ∎